Buying Time

Buying Time

The Foundations of the Electronic Church

Peter Elvy

TWENTY-THIRD PUBLICATIONS
Mystic, Connecticut

Acknowledgements

Excerpt from *Cosmos* by Carl Sagan (Ballantine Science) © Random House Inc, 201 East 50th Street, New York, NY 10022, USA. Permission for non-exclusive use in the English language throughout the World given by Scott Meredith Literary Agency Inc, 845 Third Avenue, New York, NY 10022, USA.

'Religion and Television: Report on Research' by William F. Fore, *The Christian Century* (July 18–25, 1984) p713.

Extract from *Religious Television—The American Experience* by Peter G. Horsfield © 1983 by Longman Group Inc, 95 Church Street, White Plains, New York, NY 10601, USA. Used with permission.

Excerpt from the *Television Awareness* training manual, edited by Ben Logan. Permission to reproduce given by United Methodist Communications, Division of Public Media, 475 Riverside Drive, Suite 1370, New York, NY 10115, USA (UMCom).

Extract from the *Washington Post*, Friday, October 18, 1985, page D.8.

Pictures of the Crystal Cathedral reproduced by courtesy of Robert Schuller Ministries, 4201 W. Chapman Ave, Orange, CA 92668, USA.

North American Edition (revised) 1987
Twenty-Third Publications
P.O. Box 180
Mystic CT 06355
(203) 536-2611

First Published in Great Britain 1986
by McCrimmon Publishing Co. Ltd.
Great Wakering, Essex, England.

ISBN 0-89622-325-6
Library of Congress Catalog Card Number 86-51540

Cover design by Paul Shuttleworth

The church tower depicted on the cover is not intended to refer to a particular church but to churches generally.

Contents

In memory of my father
R M ELVY
Milwaukee newsman

Foreword

*The Rev Dr Hans Florin, General Secretary,
World Association for Christian Communication,
1976–86.*

Buying and selling religion is not new. The mighty
throughout the ages have bought religion to reinforce their interests. And religion has been and still
is for sale so that it may dwell comfortably in the
houses of power. Yet, such religion stands dis-
owned by Christ.

It should not come as a surprise that in these days
of globe-spanning mass communication air-time for
religion also is bought and sold. The deregulation of
broadcasting—first in the USA and now increasingly in Europe, and, indeed, in all continents—paves
the way for private and commercial broadcasting.
Deregulation decrees the competition to customary
public networks to be a virtue.

● *Dr Hans Florin*

Commercial broadcasting lives by selling airtime. And where religious programmes seek to buy
this air-time, two lucrative interests meet and com-
plement each other. Today the media market place
is big business—and religion is an integral part of
it.

Peter Elvy portrays this media religion. It is to
his credit that he does so under the fitting title
of *Buying Time*. He explores, eminently readably,
the phenomenon of the 'Electronic Church'. He
does so as journalist, religious broadcaster and
priest. The journalist and broadcaster stands in awe
of the truly gigantic achievements of the televangelists. The priest probes the Electronic Church, by
which definition media religion is commonly
known.

Peter Elvy, both priest and journalist, presents

this portrait at a time at which media religion, 'made in the USA', stands poised to tempt the faithful all around the globe. His portrait is kind, full of sympathy for the pioneers who set out to make Jesus known among all peoples. His brush paints both lights and shadows—the lights of admiration and the shadows of caution.

The journalist admires the skill and courage of the televangelist pioneers in their daring to adopt mass medium TV. The priest cannot ignore that this powerful medium also adopts, coerces the pioneers. The pioneers for Jesus-of-the-airwaves become pioneers of the very media power they so confidently, so innocently, sought to harness. Their personalities grow beyond all reasonable people proportions. The Jesus they profess to proclaim withstood temptation precisely because his ministry was devoid of power.

Peter Elvy concludes that media religion is, indeed, 'electronic', adjusting to and skilfully exploiting all the rules and temptations governing television—but that is not the Church. However, he cannot spare the churches the reproach of having vacated too easily the statutory space in public broadcasting that is theirs to fill, to use with skill and imagination. It is, therefore, these very churches who are the prime target of this book. This book is for them—for all of us who live, practise our faith and minister in them. This book is particularly a challenge to the churches in Europe at a time when they should be alert to the 'Electronic Church' and when they still can avert its tempting message of personal comfort.

Jesus was not for sale. His church must not be for sale—despite past lapses to the contrary. Peter Elvy has bought time for the churches by unmasking the temptation which is inherent in buying time for religion in the global media market-place.

Preface

Many people made it possible for me to watch television in America. Chelmsford Diocese and Essex Radio gave me encouragement, time and financial support. More help with the high cost of visiting 20 states of the Union came from the Hockerill Educational Foundation, the Jerusalem Trust, the Essex Churches' Local Radio Committee, the Sandford St Martin Trust, the Harold Buxton Trust, the Church of England's Board for Mission and Unity and the parishes of Great Burstead and Shenfield. I thank the Bishop of Bradwell, the Right Reverend Derek Bond, for his support and enthusiasm for the project.

My journeyings now add up to 40,000 miles; and for me they would have been quite impossible but for the kindness and courtesy of so many communicators. Without the encouragement of my publisher, Joan McCrimmon, and the help of Dr Hans Florin of the World Association for Christian Communication, this book could not have been written. Also I thank Bishop Agnellus Andrew, Dr William Fore (New York), the Bishop of Peterborough, Dr Ben Armstrong (New Jersey), Mr Karl Holtznider (Los Angeles), Mr Sebastian Temple and Miss Karen Dardick (Los Angeles), the Rev Leonard Freeman (New York), Mr and Mrs William Bauhan (New Hampshire), the Rev John Barton, Mr Rupert Neve, Mr Russell Shaw (Washington), Rev John Geaney (Washington), Dr Curtis Chambers (Shreveport), Rev David Beer, Mr David Falkus, Mr Nelson Price (New York), Mr Charles Cordle, Mrs Audrey Landon (Phoenix), Mr Sen Kolla (Phoenix), Dr Charles Roden (Fort Worth), Mr Jeff

Bonser, Mr Eddy Frankland, Dr David Clarke (Virginia Beach), Canon Richard Anderson (New York), Dr Robert Browne, Mr Tony Black, the Rev Eric Shegog, Mr Alan Hockley, and Multipoint Communications Ltd.

I acknowledge my great debt to 'X', a perceptive Christian 'mole'. 'X' showed me both the greatness and wretchedness of the Electronic Church. I have had the best of guides, and if I lose my way in America it is my fault entirely.

On my journeys I have had to acquire a new language. 'Cherry-picking', 'bicycling', 'piggy-backing' and other strange expressions and acronyms are mixed with English in this book. A glossary is provided on Page 153.

For 14 months my wife Petra has had to live with *Buying Time*, keeping me company on some of my American journeys and listening patiently to many ideas. I am grateful also to Mrs Anne Miles for interpreting my hieroglyphics and typing the manuscript. Last but not least I thank our American in-laws, Bob and Elly (Dr and Mrs Oudemans).

Speaking in the 1985 debate on whether or not to allow cameras into the House of Commons, Joe Ashton, the telegenic Labour MP for Bassetlaw, lambasted television as the destroyer of football, the cinema and religion. I agree with him. My own religious broadcasting is confined to radio. The risks to religion are lower; and anyway, as the little boy said, 'the scenery is better'.

Peter Elvy,
Great Burstead, Essex,
1986.

Chapter 1

Noisy planet

'*But is there anyone out there to talk to? With a third or half a trillion stars in our Milky Way Galaxy alone, could ours be the only one accompanied by an inhabited planet? How much more likely it is that technical civilizations are a cosmic commonplace, that the Galaxy is pulsing and humming with advanced societies, and, therefore, that the nearest such culture is not so very far away—perhaps transmitting from antennas established on a planet of a naked-eye star just next door. Perhaps when we look up at the sky at night, near one of those faint pinpoints of light is a world in which someone quite different from us is then glancing idly at a star we call the Sun and entertaining, for just a moment, an outrageous speculation.*'—Carl Sagan, *Cosmos.*

Imagine a spaceship. It has come nearer to our Sun than to any other star in the Milky Way. It has come from far away in the galaxy, from a civilisation more advanced than any of ours. The ship has come in peace and the reason for the immense journey through space is quite simply curiosity. If the crew find intelligent life, they do not intend to make contact or even reveal their presence. In a matter of earth-seconds, the spaceship's scanners reveal that our own blue planet is the solar system's only source of non-accidental radio. The crew of the spaceship are more than interested. Electro-magnetic radiation lights up the entire universe, sometimes in stupendous bursts, but it's not every day that they discover a planet where intelligent beings have learned to tame this power and use it to communicate.

The spaceship comes from a world which has conquered disease and no longer finds challenge in technology. Problems of supply and demand were solved long ago. Their last frontier, the remaining question, is what we on Planet Earth call Theology. They have realised that even their superb science can lead them only some of the way to the source of the Cosmos. When they parked their ship in the orbit of our Sun, they were certain they could learn nothing from us about the origin and working of the universe. However, they do have a profound interest in our religions.

By Earth's twentieth-century standards, the spaceship's electronic equipment is superlative. Of course, not every broadcast of ours can break out into space. Long, medium and many short wavelengths are reflected back to Planet Earth by its ionisphere. However, very high frequency radio (VHF) and television races out into space, and our broadcasts, travelling at a speed of 300,000 kilometres per second, are received by the spaceship almost at once. Signals from any location on Earth can be deciphered and understood. No matter what language is used, every reference to God can be analysed. The immense resources of a great civilisation have been placed behind this project. The crew of the spaceship have just one question to answer: What are the peoples of planet Earth broadcasting about their God?

From their experience of other planets, the crew know all about night and day on Earth. They are unsurprised by the discovery that human beings spend one third of their lives unconscious. Average patterns of sleep, work and leisure are soon worked out and it becomes obvious that Earth's public broadcasting audiences vary enormously in size. Prime-time TV is clearly the planet's most powerful medium, and perhaps the key to its collective values. Therefore it is to prime-time TV that the ship directs its sensors and on which the ship's theologians focus their attention. They are soon provided with an overview.

The USSR is the Earth's largest political unit. Broadcasting is closely controlled by an atheist government. Despite large Moslem and Christian populations, God has no place on Soviet television. Indeed, belief in God is actively discouraged.

One quarter of the planet's population are Chinese; and the People's Republic is another atheist state. There is no religious broadcasting, but government spokesmen speak respectfully of the Three Selfs Movement—a coalition of patriotic Christians.

India has the second of the planet's great populations and its largest democracy. It has a modern educational satellite television service. It is not difficult to detect a strong and ancient Hindu culture to which the idea of religious broadcasting seems unnecessary. Indian dance, drama and music are rooted in religion, and of course constitute a large part of the country's 'secular' broadcasting.

South America is a nominally Christian region with a huge Catholic population and a vocal and fast-growing Protestant minority. Latin America is undergoing political change, urbanisation and, in places, revolution. Television is controlled by governments of either Left or Right. There are exceptions to the rule, but active Catholics tend to be unpopular with all governments.

Forecasters see Japan and the Pacific as the planet's future economic centre. Most television equipment is manufactured in the region but the main influence on programmes is North American. The ancient religions, with their emphasis on contemplation, have little in common with television.

Many African and Asian countries have only limited television facilities. TV receivers are not widely distributed. Most of the states have one-party constitutions or are ruled by military regimes, and television is an arm of government.

In some areas, Moslem and Christian numbers are increasing.

The Arab states and Iran have a growing television service. Much of it is paid for by oil wealth; and powerful, sometimes strident, programmes give the Moslem countries government-sponsored religious broadcasting. From Morocco to Pakistan (and even Soviet-controlled Afghanistan) the message of the Quran is clearly broadcast in prime time. Often it is difficult to distinguish between religious and political themes. In the Iran of the Mullahs, television is an important means of government control.

Western Europe was once the centre of the world, and is where Hertz discovered radio, Marconi developed it and Baird introduced television. Europe has a bewildering variety of broadcasting systems. Many people speak of a 'post-Christian' situation. The still-religious minority continue to hold many of the levers of power. Prime-time television is almost entirely light entertainment, and at least 30 per cent of programmes are North American. The tradition of public service in broadcasting is strong and some governments frown on direct television evangelism. In Scandinavia, Germany and Britain, there is well-organised co-operation between public broadcasting and the established churches.

The United States of America, the richest and most powerful nation on earth, is the source of the overwhelming proportion of its television output. The country has 1,181 television stations serving 84,000,000 'television households'. Nearly 40 per cent of homes in the USA receive television from one of 10,000 cable systems, which are in turn served by one or more of the USA's 21 broadcast satellites. In their offices on New York's Avenue of the Americas, the TV networks and programme makers reach decisions which influence the viewing habits of the entire planet. Religious broadcasting, much of it at prime time, flourishes. Each year, billions of dollars change hands as Christians buy time on the airwaves.

The nation's fourth biggest national television network is a religious enterprise. Preaching superstars are watched by millions and even influence the politics of the nation. Many large and medium-sized churches are permanently equipped for television broadcasting.

Back on board the spaceship, the electronic processors are no longer working under maximum load. The computers have delivered their averages and analyses. Planet Earth's crescendo of prime-time television is mainly light entertainment. It continues to race out into space, and in a hundred years or so will no doubt be the talk of the galaxy or even one of the Milky Way's minor scandals. The greater part of this television traffic is North American; and it includes a lively, sometimes boisterous religious component.

The spaceman/theologian is beginning to find an answer. God gets far more TV time in the United States than anywhere else on earth, and his market share is said to be growing. In some years his followers have paid $500 million to bring his message to the screen. Back on board the spaceship, the viewers are sampling Planet Earth's religious television. 'Dial-flipping' may well bring them an ayatollah, but if they restrict their options to Christian programming they will almost certainly find a North American televangelist. His name will probably be one of these: Pat Robertson, Jim Bakker, Jerry Falwell, Robert Schuller, Jimmy Swaggart, John Giminez, Kenneth Copeland, John Osteen, Marilyn Hickey, Paul Crouch, Oral Roberts, Richard Roberts, Mother Angelica, Richard De Haan, James Robinson, James Kennedy, David Mainse, Jack Van Impe, Bob Tilton, Fred Price and Charles F. Stanley.

These names are at the top of a religious broadcasting industry. Some are superstars, others are gaining or losing stature. With two interesting exceptions, all would describe their Christianity by one of six different but overlapping Protestant adjectives: evangelical, born-again, Bible-believing, charismatic, fundamentalist, conservative. Most belong to a well organised trade association, National Religious Broadcasters (NRB) with its own statement of faith, code of ethics and financial principles and guidelines. Most would use state-of-the-art broadcasting equipment, including satellite uplinks. Many have created impressive, even stupendous, institutions.

The Broadcasters' buildings include the Crystal Cathedral, the Cathedral of Tomorrow, Thomas Road Baptist Church in Lynchburg, Virginia, Liberty University, CBN University, The City of Faith Hospital, Oral Roberts University and PTL's Heritage USA. Most have an international emphasis in their ministry, and some are well known in Australia, South-East Asia, even Europe and the Middle East. All, without exception, concentrate on

• *The Crystal Cathedral, Garden Grove, California*

speech. They stand in the tradition of the American revivalist camp meeting.

Television enables the preaching to become eyeball-to-eyeball communication—one way at least. The evangelists are, or course, individuals with very different personalities and styles. They are of necessity businessmen and rely on others, almost always the viewers, to provide the huge sums necessary to buy TV time.

Television does not give them much flexibility. Their programmes conform to two or three well-proved formats, but none of them is dull. Certainly some are 'ruffle-shirted and pink-tuxedoed men' but most are sober-suited. With Bible in hand, and helped by a host of lesser, local lights, they power North America's 'Electronic Church'.

The spacemen have one answer. Planet Earth's Christian television is largely North American and Protestant, and it is embedded in an entertainment and communications industry that is acutely com-mercialised. It is the barest of answers. But let us now leave the spaceship to go on its way while we come down to Earth to the God-fearing America where 47 per cent of the population take some part in this Electronic Church while 42 per cent partici-pate in the real thing.

Chapter 2

The Almighty's dollar

His immaculately tailored slacks and contrasting monogrammed jacket give him the look of a successful tennis coach. She sits beside him attacking middle age from under a hive of platinum curls that would have delighted Louis Quatorze. The camera carefully notices that they are holding hands. Her mood changes quickly. She laughs often and cries easily. Sometimes she is so moved that her voice becomes just a squeak. She backs him up with 'Praise the Lord' and 'Amen' while he does most of the talking.

'There is coming a time when all the satellites will be linked together and the whole world will hear the voice of God.' The man on the screen is more than a TV host. He is more than a preacher or a Bible teacher. Trinity Broadcasting Network is on the air, and Paul Crouch is its president. He is sharing a glimpse of the future. The time is short. The Lord is coming soon. Space technology is going to put the Gospel on the screens of many nations. TBN is part of that process. Paul Crouch is proud of his hardware and often talks about it to his viewers.

Outside in the bright Californian sunshine stands an 18-wheeled mobile monster. He calls it the Holy Beamer. It tooks mighty enough to carry a missile, but on its back sits a huge satellite uplink dish. Computer-controlled, it waits under its coat of gleaming paint to trundle to yet another broadcast location, to spurt its next salvo of Live Praise to the satellite waiting 35,000 kilometres above. Paul Crouch often talks and writes to his supporters about satellites and the time when he made the first-ever satellite link-up from the top of the Mount of

Olives. 'High in the midst of heaven a drama so immense is taking place that Satan and all of hell is
reeling from the impact. The Prince of the Power of
the Air is no longer the undisputed Prince. A new
invasion beachhead has been launched into the airwaves! Praise the Lord. ANGEL II is in orbit; that
tiny-winged piece of electronic miracle is picking up
"Let's Just Praise the Lord". Twenty-four hours a
day Christian Television is now raining down on
half the Western Hemisphere.'

Paul Crouch, broadcaster and businessman for
God, sees himself a part of a divine plan to spread
the word that the King will soon be here. 'The
Good News simply is: WE ARE GOING TO
MAKE IT! Though demons and devils roar,
though friends misunderstand, though mountains
stand in our way—we will, will GO, GO, GO 'til
Jesus comes! Will you go with us to see this glorious
vision of Christian Television through to a glorious
VICTORY? I know you will! Jan and I will never
turn back either. Someday we will stand side by
side before the Great Judgement Seat for believers
and will hear Jesus say—Well done, good and faithful servants. Deep in my spirit I believe that before

● *Salvoes of praise:*
the Holy Beamer

another ten years pass we will be rejoicing around the throne of God.'

Some preliminary rejoicing is already appropriate at TBN's Tustin headquarters. The network is expanding and is taken by cable systems in many parts of the US. It also owns a chain of over-the-air television stations, including a mighty five million-watt transmitter in Miami. In Nevis/St Christopher, TBN is building the first 24-hour Christian television station in the Caribbean. The finger of God is seen in every step forward that the network takes: 'After four years of intense spiritual battle, the airwaves over Oklahoma were permeated with the oil of the Holy Spirit. Over one thousand souls were saved that night as Channel 14 came on air with one hundred per cent Christian programming for the first time in Oklahoma history.' Crouch's language is apocalyptic and in sharp contrast to the plush studio set, with its warm antiques, easy chairs, stained glass window and glossy grand piano. Jan and Paul preside over *Praise the Lord*, a host show interspersed with gospel music and video clips. Interviews end with prayer in which the viewer is invited to share.

In the technical language of Christianity, Paul and Jan Crouch are charismatics. They claim that ten years of miracles have put them where they are. They see the end of the age approaching, and their emphasis is on the gifts and guidance of the Spirit of God. Their apocalyptic message is gift-wrapped in a Hollywood package (in 1982 Jan Crouch received the Golden Halo Award—bronze division). Their style seems to owe more to Liberace than to Revelation. Not yet in the front pew of the Electronic Church, and too sugary for many tastes, the charismatic, coiffured Crouches wait serenely for the End, and in the meantime improve their electronics and build up their network. But in a hardbitten, professional world, they are well spoken of by their peers for their generosity with free air time for religious good causes.

No-one could call Jimmy Swaggart sugary. He too is a charismatic. Entertainment is in the family

(Jerry Lee Lewis and Mickey Gilley are his cousins), but Brother Swaggart is no comedian. With jabbing finger, and holding his glasses for safety, he presents an uncompromising definition of a Spirit-filled, Bible-believing church. He is no great recruiting sergeant for the traditional churches. He's against 'ecclesiastical liturgical religiosity'. He believes that 'the church world that has rejected the baptism of the Holy Spirit is useless'. Swaggart is at his best in large gatherings. He loosens his tie and prowls up and down like a caged cat. He can bring a crowd of thousands to their feet.

• *Jimmy Swaggart: rising star*

He is the rising star of the Electronic Church. His television presence is compelling, but not especially warm. He is first and foremost an orator, with the Southern habit of building in pauses for the listeners to fill. He claims a weekly viewing audience of ten million in the United States. Worldwide, his programmes are aired in eleven languages. He has made 46 albums and his press release describes him as 'the most popular Gospel music artist in history'. As far as time-buying is concerned, Jimmy Swaggart's spending power is the envy of other, longer established TV preachers. The heart of his widespread activities is the World Ministry Center in Baton Rouge, Louisiana. Located on a 180-acre site, the Jimmy Swaggart headquarters includes a 7,000-seat church and the Vance Teleproduction Center, renowned for its commitment to language translation.

Swaggart tries to break free from televised evangelism's limited range of programme formats. He appears sometimes with a back-up panel of studio experts. The experiment does not make for great television. There is a lack of clarity about his role. Is he the chairman? Are the experts on the show simply to add weight to his message? Jimmy Swaggart is most effective out on the boards and with the audience cheering, but with the TV cameras giving close-ups of the deadpan, wry expressions that would otherwise be lost.

Named in two *Good Housekeeping* polls as the second most influential man in the United States,

• *Jerry Falwell:
influential*

Jerry Falwell is known worldwide as the founder of Moral Majority, the since-renamed Washington-based pressure group for right-wing causes. Falwell's friends include President Reagan, the Republic of South Africa and the State of Israel. He travels 8,000 miles a week and is not one to duck an argument, whether it is with jeering Harvard students or a more polite but nonetheless hostile Oxford Union. He is a national politician and quite an important one, but his base and his proudest achievement is in his home town of Lynchburg, Virginia. His Thomas Road Church, now the second biggest Baptist church in the country, has grown so much that it is now in its third building. It is here each Sunday morning, jammed with TV directors and electronic hardware, that Falwell tapes *Old Time Gospel Hour*. Each Sunday evening the show is broadcast to 392 stations across the country, and 62 telephone operators stand by to receive incoming pledges.

Jerry Falwell's empire needs $100 million a year just to keep going. A huge sum is needed to buy TV time, and in 1984 he put $30 million into Liberty University in Lynchburg, the apple of his eye. He has 2,200 employees. He hopes his 261 baby adoption clinics will eventually swell to 10,000. He carries accident insurance for $105 million. On some moral issues he makes common cause with Catholics, Jews and Mormons. Once known for bursts of pulpit sarcasm, his style has mellowed. His pride in Liberty University is there on the screen for all to see. The financial commitments of his city-state are enormous and long-term. With his political involvement, albeit Right-wing, in Washington and Pretoria, he has to work hard to reassure his supporters nationwide that he is still a homespun fundamentalist.

Most of the TV preachers would call themselves evangelical Christians. Under this broad Protestant banner, many would wear another badge: charismatic, meaning 'Spirit-led'; and fundamentalist, meaning 'Bible-believing.' The two terms overlap, and indeed charismatics and fundamentalists can be found right across the Christian spectrum. Nevertheless, the words mean something. Jimmy Swaggart calls himself a charismatic. He asks his audience to pray for the New Testament gifts of prophecy and tongues. Jerry Falwell is a fundamentalist, a term which in the pre-war liberal Protestant heyday was far from being a compliment. He is the proud publisher of the *Fundamentalist Magazine*.

Within the broad evangelical tide, there are other, more idiosyncratic currents. Some of the televangelists emphasise success in life and business as signs of God's blessing. Interestingly, Jimmy Swaggart and Jerry Falwell do not echo the prosperity theme. But Bob Tilton, a Dallas pastor and a rising star in the electronic firmament, preaches a rags-to-riches gospel. God wants his followers to be wealthy and successful and to achieve promotion at work. Oral Roberts, next to Billy Graham the biggest name in the American evangelical world uses the tele-blessing, 'May God bless you in your bodies, in your spirits and in your finances'.

Oral Roberts has always been a much more controversial figure than Billy Graham. By the 1950s he was nationally known as a healer. Television extended his healing ministry by thousands of miles to countless sick viewers. Some were shocked by what they regarded as showbiz religion playing on helpless gullibility. Others claimed to be healed by this newly available television sacrament. Roberts changed his style in the mid-1960s. He ended the exhausting round of tent crusades, and this in turn dried up the source of most of his television material. He concentrated on radio evangelism, and on the university which bears his name in Tulsa. In 1969, as president of ORU, he returned to the screens with a glamorous new show which became America's top-ranking syndicated religious programme.

The Roberts' impact on Tulsa, Oklahoma, can only really be appreciated from the air. ORU is now a fully accredited university. Its graduate schools, housed in futuristic buildings, produce ministers, doctors, dentists and communicators. The students call it 'the campus that landed'. The City of Faith Hospital is housed in three gleaming, high-rise towers. Television studios are in constant use for the Roberts TV shows of father and son.

Like all the major television apostles, Oral Roberts is faced with the problem of ensuring the apostolic succession. Jerry Falwell has a 45-minute tape locked in a vault in Lynchburg revealing his plans for the succession. Robert H. Schuller's son, Robert A, is senior pastor of the Schuller Ministries' Rancho Capistrano Community Church. Pat Robertson's eldest son Timothy is CBN's executive vice-president for broadcasting and video enterprises. On Paul Crouch's TBN, several youth-oriented programmes have featured Paul Crouch Jr. Oral Roberts has no inhibitions about the future. He is going to be succeeded by his son Richard; and about that in Tulsa there is absolutely no doubt.

Richard Roberts has his own show. He too claims healing insights which are available to the television

● *'The Campus that Landed': The Roberts complex in Tulsa*

audience. His daily show is bright. He bounces on with all the loose-elbowed confidence of a screen star. He takes a microphone and, accompanied by the brass of one of ORU's orchestras, sings expertly. Holding hands with wife Lindsay—his first, and equally televised, marriage to Patti ended in divorce—he presides over a glittery show that is from the same mould as many 'secular' host shows. But the vocabulary is far removed from secular programmes. The marriage to Lindsay was 'ordained by God'. Richard is going to Northern Ireland for three days, and tomorrow on the show he will be 'anointed' for the task. Today on the show is a very special guest, their own 'miracle' baby Jordan.

One of the biggest names in the Electronic Church is Robert Schuller. Every Sunday morning his *Hour of Power* is broadcast from the Crystal Cathedral in Garden Grove, Los Angeles. A truly beautiful building, it contains many wonders. Against acres of glass stands the world's largest pipe organ. Beside the preacher is a Sony Jumbotron, a monster TV screen bigger than a house. There are ten voice choirs, two bell choirs, various instrumental ensembles and a symphony orchestra. As if this were not enough, there are canaries in cages and fountains that tinkle. This great church deserves to be called a cathedral. It's a long way up from the drive-in cinema where Robert Schuller started, but the message is the same—and it is a message of optimism.

Schuller stands apart from the other TV preachers. It is difficult to bracket him with the evangelicals. His message, like his cathedral, is bright, flower-filled and full of the power of positive thinking. Norman Vincent Peale has been the determining influence on Schuller. He in turn gives PT a West Coast glow and has translated it for television. 'God loves you and so do I' is his greeting. From the Sermon on the Mount he extracts the BE-HAPPY-ATTITUDES. Schuller is brilliantly telegenic, and the Jumbotron now allows him to wink and raise an eyebrow to his four thousand congregation as well. He publishes a special *Possibility Thinker's Bible*. He is aware of the constant criticism that his message falls somewhat short of a Christ-centred gospel. He would claim that he meets people where they are, to lead them to the cross; and he has many supporters in the traditional churches. But the uneasy feeling persists that the teaching of this warm, witty, twinkling-eyed man would be just as acceptable in a Rotarian's handbook. Or would it? Schuller is an enigma, and from Sunday to Sunday there are subtle differences in the *Hour of Power*.

Much depends on his special guest. If he or she is an articulate evangelical, Schuller will catch the mood and even develop it. But with the President of the Boy Scouts of America, the theme is one of Service, Patriotism and Loyalty. His composition *I Am the American Flag* received an award in 1973 as 'the most outstanding sermon in the United States'. 'It is my positive answer to the negative thinkers who deluge us with cynical, phony, pessimistic predictions that would discredit America and the values that make her great.'

Dr Schuller and his family have not escaped pain or crippling injury. His supporters would say his message is salvation-centred but attractively packaged for the twentieth century. Lt Col Henry Gariepy, editor-in-chief of the American Salvation Army's *Warcry* magazine, is warm in his praise: 'I have derived personal inspiration from Dr Schuller. Some state that he does not bring the cross into his television preachment, but I have listened carefully and have found that there is a central emphasis on salvation by Jesus Christ and the ministry of the Holy Spirit in our Christian life. I think he is doing what Dietrich Bonhoeffer challenged us to do, to speak of God in a secular way.'

There is a great variation in style and purpose between the major television preaching stars but, Robert Schuller excepted, their front rank stands firmly in the American evangelical tradition. This fact alone means that the Electronic Church can be in no way representative of the North American denominational mix formed by wave after wave of transatlantic migrants.

It has taken the greatest transfer of people in human history to populate the American continent. The result is a nation of nations: Irish, Polish, African, Vietnamese, Mexican. The American nation is made up from the other peoples of the world, and Europeans are heavily represented. From pre-Revolutionary days, every European Christian variation has rooted itself in American soil. Quakers, Congregationalists, Unitarians, Methodists, Catholics, Lutherans, Baptists, Orthodox and dozens more. And most survive.

In the 1930s, Bonhoeffer commented that 'it had been granted to the Americans less than any other nation to realise the visible unity of the Church of God'. The denominational mix is startling, and made even more colourful by the later addition of several neo-Christian, home-grown varieties, of which Latter Day Saints, Christian Scientists and Jehovah's Witnesses are the most successful.

By far the largest church in the United States are the Roman Catholics, with 52 million members. The Southern Baptists are the biggest Protestant denomination (14 million members), followed by the United Methodist Church (9,300,000). There are eight million Lutherans; and among the many smaller denominations are the Episcopalians (2,700,000). It is always possible to argue statistics, but there is common agreement on some points. The Catholic Church in the USA is neither growing nor shrinking (although it is failing to hold the allegiance of large numbers of Mexican immigrants). The 'mainline' Protestant churches—those that belong to the National Council of Churches—have lost members until very recently, while those who would call themselves evangelicals have increased in numbers. However, within American Christianity as a whole they are clearly a minority.

Now it might be reasonable to expect that religious broadcasting should broadly reflect the religious arithmetic of the country. But that is certainly not the case. The traditional churches still enjoy

*Broadcasting ≠
prop'l to denomnat°*

some free access to broadcasting, but often early in the morning or late at night. 'A new meaning for Alpha and Omega!' according to one broadcaster. Salvationists, Catholics, Orthodox, Methodists, Lutherans, Congregationalists, Disciples of Christ, even the Southern Baptists (the denomination rather than individuals) are under-represented in public broadcasting.

The leading lights in the Electronic Church do not represent the churches, and indeed they do not occupy themselves with denominational concerns. With the exception of Robert Schuller and the lone Catholic, Mother Angelica, they are clearly identified with the fundamentalist and charismatic movements, which, although strong, are nevertheless minorities within American Christendom. With only a few exceptions, they own and operate their own broadcasting institutions, which are free from denominational control or investment. Robert Schuller has his huge Crystal Cathedral. Oral Roberts has made a stupendous investment in real estate. All these facilities were built on broadcasting; and the list could be a long one. Robertson, Humbard, Swaggart, Falwell—they all have or had their own centres of worship and broadcasting. Many have building programmes in the Third World, and there is nothing owed to the traditional churches or indeed to any other institutions. One of the televangelists' proudest boasts is, 'It's all paid for'.

There are some apparent exceptions. Robert Schuller is an accredited minister of the Reformed Church in America; but his beautiful cathedral has his warm personality stamped all over. Oral Roberts, in a much-publicised move, accepted local eldership in the United Methodist Church. There has been much speculation about this dramatic gesture. Unkind observers saw it as a cynical move to extend the Oral Roberts 'donor base' into a large mainline church. They do not understand their man. The sudden conversion to Methodism was a typically flamboyant thank-offering to the United Methodist Church for its official conference approv-

al of the charismatic movement. The courtship has
not led to a marriage. The Roberts headquarters in
Tulsa makes it abundantly clear that the evangelist
has in no way deserted his old followers. There is
now no discernible link between the Oral Roberts
Evangelistic Association and world Methodism.

Mother Angelica, the most visible Roman Catholic in the Electronic Church, is in no way an official
Catholic representative. Her Eternal World Television Network, based in Birmingham, Alabama, relies on donations from viewers and well-wishers.
Her television style is folksy and without frills, but
she stands for a conservative Catholicism that is
now out of favour with the hierarchy.

The high priests of the Electronic Church are
their own men. They owe nothing to the majority
churches. And indeed they have largely displaced
them on America's 84 million screens. The uneasy
frontier between evangelicalism and the mainline
churches is an imaginary line found somewhere
within the huge Southern Baptist denomination. In
this church, two approaches to religious broadcasting can be seen side by side. Prominent ministers
such as Dr Charles F. Stanley, a former President of
the Southern Baptist Convention, have their own
personal niche in the Electronic Church. Meanwhile at the Church's Radio and Television Commission in Fort Worth, Texas, there is an expensive
denominational effort to launch a national religious
television network. Also, the relatively small (and
perhaps not 'mainline') Lutheran Missouri Synod
has a long and very effective record in broadcasting.

Nevertheless, the great majority of American
churchgoers are unrepresented in the Electronic
Church. Prime-time religious television is in the
hands of independent entrepreneurs. They buy
their own time and are reimbursed by the viewer/
disciple. They achieved their ascendancy because
the mainline churches relied from the beginning on
free time provided by the broadcasting companies.
When the free time disappeared, the churches too
began to disappear from the screens.

The independents have had luck or God on their

side. Satellite technology married to cable television has encouraged so-called Christian networks. Toll-free long-distance telephone privileges and ever more personal word processors have enabled the TV stars to keep in touch with their supporters. As far as broadcasting is concerned, the mainliners are now on the side of the tracks. It was not always so.

● *Inside the Crystal Cathedral: 90ft doors admit drive-in worshippers.*

Chapter 3

West Side story

On Manhattan's Upper West Side, on the high ground overlooking the Hudson River, is set the man-made mountain that is Riverside Church. This interdenominational Protestant church takes some of its architectural features from Chartres Cathedral. With its carillon tower and Superman statue of the Angel Gabriel blowing his trumpet, it is too massively proportioned to be beautiful. It was built by John D. Rockefeller Jnr. For the first 20 years of its existence its minister was Harry Emerson Fosdick. He had begun his preaching ministry in a Presbyterian pulpit, but in 1925, under fundamentalist pressure, he withdrew. Riverside Church has been a stronghold of the liberal, free-thinking tradition in Protestantism, and is now also something of a centre for liberal political causes.

Separated from the church by Riverside Drive, but still dwarfed by its cliff-like walls, is Union Theological Seminary. This institution for the training of ministers was founded in 1938 by 'new school' Presbyterians for men 'of moderate views' of any denomination. From the beginning it has allowed critical studies of the Biblical texts and encouraged toleration.

Standing beside Riverside Church, across Rheinhold Niebuhr Place, is a 19-storey structure sheathed in Alabama limestone and known variously as The Interchurch Centre, 475 Riverside Drive, 475, and The God Box. It occupies an entire city block. The land on which it stands was made available by John D. Rockefeller Jnr. He gave the first $2 million to the building fund and, liking limestone, met the entire costs of the exterior facing.

The building is now valued at well over $50 million.

475 is a visible symbol of the twentieth-century movement that has brought so many of the mainline churches closer together. It is an ecumenical tower, and in its office suites are housed the secretariats of many denominations. Among the tenants are the African Methodist Episcopal Church, the United Church of Christ, the Reformed Church in America and nearly 30 more. With 460,000 square feet of office space, 182 miles of electrical wiring, underground parking and a cafeteria serving a thousand lunches daily, 475 Riverside Drive is the Central Station of mainline American Protestantism. Inevitably it serves as the headquarters of the National Council of Churches, which consists of 32 Protestant and Orthodox churches and a total of 40 million members. Its full-length title is the National Council of the Churches of Christ in the USA.

Dr Willam Fore is a very senior official of the NCCC. As one of its six assistant general secretaries, he directs the communications commission. He deals with the major US broadcasting networks, with industry and with the US Government. He is a minister of the United Methodist Church, a hiker, an author and a film maker. He is also President of the influential London-based World Association for Christian Communication. If the mainline American churches have a spokesman on broadcasting, he is William Fore.

He is more than an ecclesiastical bureaucrat. He asks questions about American religious broadcasting and, more important still, about broadcasting itself. Fundamentalist broadcasters respect him. For the non-fundamentalists he is a standard-bearer. In a stream of books, lectures and magazine articles, the influential Dr Fore advocates a new task for the churches. He is less concerned with regaining the air time lost to the fundamentalists, but more interested in alerting the churches to the mind-bending power of television. He disapproves of the electronic preachers not so much because they have ousted him and his friends from the air-waves, but because they have rushed headlong into

● *Ecumenical tower:*
475 Riverside Drive

the two-dimensional country of television-land and maybe lost a dimension of the Christian gospel on the way.

In 1984, in *The Christian Century*, he put forward the idea that *general* television had now taken over many of the functions historically belonging to the church: 'Television, not the church, now communicates what is going on outside the parish, telling us how to behave, what to wear, who has power and who is powerless, what to believe about the world and what is ultimate value. In this sense, general television, far more than religious television, is the Church's real competitor.' For William Fore, and many of the other communications experts in 475, the urgent task for the churches is to train Christians to survive television, and above all to teach parishioners how to cope with the 'enormous wave of exciting, soporific, entertaining, debasing, informative, misleading phenomena that enters their homes on an average of seven hours a day, every day'.

In 475 Riverside Drive, the emphasis now is on viewer survival, media reform, television awareness training and conserving the Christian species. Some of the poachers have turned into gamekeepers! Nevertheless the displacement of the mainline churches by evangelical broadcasters has not been by voluntary abdication. Nor has it been a long drawn-out process. For much of the North American broadcasting era, the mainline churches had a strong position and even, according to the evangelicals, a stranglehold.

The very first religious broadcast in American history came from the parish of a mainline denomination. On the first Sunday evening of 1921, the service of Evening Prayer was transmitted from Calvary Episcopal Church, Pittsburg, on station KDKA. The broadcast was arranged by a Westinghouse Corporation engineer who sang in the Calvary Church Choir; and the Rector singularly failed to make his very own step-for-mankind mark in the history books. He was too busy to conduct the service, and asked his assistant minister to deputise for him.

This stands in stark contrast to the first non-denominational church service, which was broadcast on station WOW of Omaha, Nebraska, the following year. The minister was R.R. Brown, of Omaha Gospel Tabernacle. During the very first broadcast a listener underwent a conversion experience and ran to the radio station to tell what had happened. Brown developed as a broadcaster, and with his regular Radio Chapel Service eventually built up a weekly audience of 500,000.

The first Christian-owned radio station came on air in 1924. It was KFUO (Keep Forward, Upward, Onward) of St Louis, Missouri, and its founder was Walter A. Maier, Professor of Hebrew at the Lutheran Church Missouri Synod's Concordia Seminary. Moody Bible Institute of Chicago opened its own station, WMBI. The inaugural broadcast was a failure because another station had been allocated the same wavelength and was also broadcasting its opening programme at the very same time.

The Federal Radio Commission was set up in 1927 and imposed stringent technical standards and strict regulation of station frequency and power. A new licensing standard was applied, based on 'public interest, convenience and necessity'. All religious stations were hard hit. In 1928 there were 60. Five years later the number had been halved. In the 1930s, evangelical programmes were heard increasingly on commercial radio stations and on the new national networks. Paul Rader was one of the very first to broadcast a religious programme coast to coast. The first religious broadcaster to buy network time was Donald Grey Barnhouse.

Radio developed in an increasingly ecumenical age. The Federal Council of Churches had been founded in 1908. Local councils of churches were encouraged to develop co-operative broadcasting. In 1925, the Greater New York Federation of Churches began *The National Radio Pulpit* on station WEAF. When that station was absorbed by NBC in 1926, *Pulpit* became the first national network religious programme. It has been on the air ever since, and one of its first preachers was Henry Emerson Fosdick.

In 1927, the Columbia Broadcasting System became America's second broadcasting network. At first both NBC and CBS sold airtime to religious broadcasters. These included the Lutheran Church Missouri Synod and the fiery Catholic, Father Charles Coughlin. Within three years, and largely because of Coughlin's controversial and political statements, there was a change of policy. Both major networks refused to sell air time for religious programmes. Instead, as a public service, the networks provided free times. Sustaining time, as public service time is known, gave the major faiths an entrée into the world of big-time broadcasting. It suited the networks to deal with reputable and broadly-based religious groups. This arrangement made life easier for everyone. Tiresome right-of-reply regulations could be avoided. The ecumenical mood of many of the churches dovetailed into the networks' need to be even-handed and comprehensive. NBC and CBS developed good working relationships with three major religious partners, the National Council of Catholic Men, the Jewish Seminary of America and the Federal Council of Churches of Christ (now the NCCC).

These arrangments persisted into the television age; and indeed they still continue. But they have lost their significance, for sustaining-time religious programmes have largely disappeared. But for almost 40 years a comfortable working arrangement between the major networks and the major faiths gave American broadcasting a mainstream tone. There was broad consensus among the major faiths, and the network managers, that religious programmes should be balanced and informative. A continuing effort should be made to reflect the diversity of American religious life.

There were many successes. The National Council of Catholic Men launched the broadcasting career of Bishop Fulton Sheen. Major television series included *Frontiers of Faith* (NBC), *Look Up and Live* (CBS), *Lamp Unto My Feet* (CBS) and *Directions* (ABC). Programme formats were varied. They included drama, worship, documentaries, discussion, music and dance. For 30 years the weekly audience for network religious television ranged as high as 15 million viewers.

The networks—great broadcasting empires carved out by broadcasting moguls William Paley and David Sarnow—have been the major forces in American broadcasting. Joined later by ABC and now by the all-news network CNN, the networks give the USA its national broadcasting service. NBC and CBS informed and entertained a continent. Their relationship with the churches was not always a cosy one, but it was reasonable. It was based in New York.

From the beginning, evangelical groups and churches felt themselves excluded from a North Eastern and mainline monopoly. They regarded broadcasting as a God-given opportunity to preach the gospel to large numbers of people. Indeed, they had begun this work in 1922, long before the networks had been born.

Feeling of rejection

There were some Protestant churches outside the FCCC which were centrally structured and able to make their own denominational arrangements with the networks. The Lutheran Church Missouri Synod has had a long-term and effective presence in both sustaining-time and bought-time broadcasting. The majority of evangelicals, however, are in the congregational tradition. The important unit is the local church. If any broadcasting is to be done, or any Christian work, for that matter, it will be on the initiative of the local church and not through some plenipotentiary in New York. If money is needed to buy time for broadcasting, it will be local money on local stations.

One of the current myths of American evangelicals is that they were excluded from early network broadcasting and forced to buy their own air time from non-network stations. This is an overstatement. Commercial religious broadcasting is older than the free-time approach. In the early 1920s, in-

Myth of Exclusion

dependent evangelists and even some denominations began buying radio time; but the networks turned away from selling religious time. It was neither appropriate nor possible for the evangelicals to change direction and benefit from this new deal for the churches. They continued to purchase local air time. Independents such as Charles E. Fuller, H.M.S. Richards and Aimee Semple McPherson put large funds into buying time. In 1942, Charles Fuller had two weekly programmes on a thousand radio stations at a cost of $35,000 a week. A number of Roman Catholic dioceses and religious orders, too, spent large sums.

American broadcasting was evolving at two levels. At the national level there was a mutually beneficial understanding between the networks and the major faiths, something which Dr. Ben Armstrong of National Religious Broadcasters describes as 'the sweetheart deal'. At local level there are many examples of religious programmes on sustaining time. But there was also a strong and growing paid-time sector.

By 1959, 53 per cent of all religious time on television was bought time. Ten years later, the sweetheart deal was still loving but no longer so productive. The admirals of the Electronic Church ruled the waves. The switchover was dramatic and swift. By 1977, 92 per cent of religious television was on air time that had been paid for. The most spectacular victory for the independent evangelists has been at the local level, where free-time religious programmes have been all but eliminated.

The networks have long since abandoned their rules against selling religious airtime. Something of the 'auld alliance' still persists. The networks' own Christmas and Easter programmes still reach more viewers than the Electronic Church. However, there is an unmistakable trend towards diminishing or at least rescheduling free-time programmes.

During the 1960s and 1970s, the growth of the Electronic Church was spectacular. Oral Roberts began his ministry in 1954 on 16 local stations. In 1968 his *Thanksgiving Special* reached 27 million people. Several of the first generation of television evangelists experienced similar growth. In his study *Religious Television: the American Experience*, Peter Horsfield researches the dramatic rise of Rex Humbard, in some ways the prototype of the TV preachers. His television ministry began in 1953 from his local church in Akron, Ohio. Over the next 13 years he built up his programme until he was able to buy time regularly on 68 stations. In 1970 the number of stations carrying Rex Humbard rose to 110. Three years later, his purchasing capability and syndication had quadrupled.

There is no single reason for the rise of the Electronic Church. No neat formula can explain such a near-total triumph. From 1960, evangelicals were able to establish their own television stations when the number of UHF-frequency licences was expanded. They had long owned radio stations, but their entry into the television station market had been delayed by a shortage of frequencies. By 1978 there were 30 religious television stations.

Expansion of UHF frequency licences

By far the greatest boost to the Electronic Church came from what William Fore describes as a 'spirit of de-regulation'. From its beginning with radio, the Federal Communications Commission had defined the 'public interest' as a reason for awarding and renewing a licence to broadcast. The airwaves were seen as the common property of the nation. Those who made use of this public asset to broadcast must pay due regard to public interests, one of which is religion. Sustaining-time religious broadcasts were seen by the FCC as part of an essential control on the free market world of broadcasting. This conviction was shared by the broadcasters of the mainline churches. They regarded the free time they were given not only as useful to the religious life of the nation, but also as their democratic right, protecting public service broadcasting from an unrestrained capitalism.

In 1960, the FCC released a statement which has transformed religious broadcasting and, more than any other act or deregulation, opened the door for the electronic evangelists. The statement made it

FCC deregulation

clear that from henceforward the FCC would make no distinction between paid-time programmes and sustaining-time programmes when evaluating a station's performance in the public interest. In other words, from now on a broadcasting station could serve the public interest with religious programmes that had been bought. The effect was soon apparent. Free time was becoming an increasingly expensive gift to the churches. The days of sustaining time were numbered. Only religious broadcasters who could pay had a future.

The FCC made two further exemptions which, intentionally or not, have worked to the great benefit of the Electronic Church. Strict regulations governing money raising have been waived, as religious programmes are not regarded as commercial programmes. Also, the FCC's fairness doctrine is not deemed to apply to a religious programme, and so there is no requirement for even-handed treatment of contentious religious issues.

It is ironic that the action of a government agency has done so much to reverse the relative positions of the mainline churches and the evangelicals. For decades, independent religious broadcasters had to dig into their own pockets, or at least persuade their listeners and viewers to dig into theirs. They resented the privileged position of the churches. The FCC decision on public service programming created a new, harsher climate in which money became the only reliable key to the studio door. Now it is the mainline churches which are on the outside looking in.

But of course Humbard, Roberts and Son, Schuller, Falwell, Swaggart, Robertson and all the rest are not just the creatures of the FCC's process of deregulation. They and their colleagues in the Electronic Church have been riding on a wave that is moving powerfully in one direction simply because another greater wave once moved even more powerfully from the opposite direction before crashing into the America of the Sixties. Those were years of trauma for the United States. The crusading certainties of the Second World War were washed

Turbulence
of 60's
TV events

away. President Eisenhower's Indian Summer
fizzled out. One abrupt change among many was
the end of the 400-year-old White Anglo-Saxon Protestant ascendancy. A Roman Catholic won the
Presidency and, more significantly, the Supreme
Court ruled that religious ceremonies in public
schools (these were, of course, Protestant ceremonies) were unconstitutional.

During the Sixties, the WASPs who had ruled
North America for so long had to come to terms
with the rhetoric of the Founding Fathers. They
had to face the fact that America was not yet *E Plur-
ibus Unum*. The racial realities were put to them
first by Martin Luther King and then, with less
charity, by Black Panthers. The traditional WASP
churches were being led in new directions. 'God is
Dead' said the influential book of Gabriel Vahanian.
The churches turned more and more to social action
as a way of reviving Him, or at least healing the
nation.

Many of the sadnesses of the Sixties were multiplied by television. The assassination of President
Kennedy, followed by the killing of Martin Luther
King, were televised spectaculars of grief. The cruel
carnage of America's longest war was brought by
television to every fireside. Television probed and
exposed the nation's doubts and depression over
Vietnam. Then Watergate—the final crucifixion by
television—left Americans battered and leaderless.
With every year, the influence of television increased. In 1950, only 4.4 million American homes
had TV sets. By 1960 this figure had been multiplied ten times. By 1980 it had doubled again.

It is difficult to say whether President Carter's
fundamentalist faith was an electoral asset or a
liability. But it is certain that, once elected, he did
much more for his co-religionists than they did for
him. The Bible-believing President gave American
fundamentalists a new cohesion and respectability.

They were no longer the lunatic fringe of American
Christianity. Politically he was from the New
South, but his religion was the old Bible faith. Fre-
quently his faith was derided as archaic and fun-

damentalist; but it was real. Jimmy Carter really believed. His religion was old-time, and enabled him to write an open letter to a newspaper supporting the Genesis account of Creation. But it also gave the Presidency a new simplicity and compassion. It is ironic that the real darling of the evangelicals and of the Electronic Church is not the deeply religious Jimmy Carter but a greater communicator, Ronald Reagan.

In the turbulent 1960s, America's Protestant empire crumbled under pressures that were political, racial and social. In the 1970s, a remnant of the empire fought back. The evangelicals, reassured by the presence of one of their own in the White House, set about regaining some of the lost ground. They saw themselves as guardians of the true American values, as heirs to the puritan tradition that had forged this nation with the soul of a church. Their ideals are both religious and political. They are conservatives. They believe in the old apple-pie values of conservative America, and they believe in strong national defences to protect those values. Several of the leading television evangelists are deeply involved in right-wing politics. For most of them, the Supreme Court decision on worship in schools is a recurring topic. All of them are fulsomely patriotic. They hark back to America's so-called roots, but they mean the roots of White Anglo-Saxon Protestantism.

By the late 1970s it appeared that America might be on the verge of a religious revival. Statistical surveys gave a different picture. The evangelicals were the only religious group who were retaining their younger members. Therefore, unlike the mainline churches, their numbers were holding up. This is some way from a nationwide 'revival' but it was and still is by far the most impressive performance of any religious grouping. Is the Electronic Church the result of the so-called 'revival' or vice versa? In 1977, both *Time* magazine and *Newsweek* explored the inter-relation between the electronic evangelists and the evangelical surge. This is a chicken-and-egg problem. The real answer lies in the viewer and

listener statistics. If it can be proved that the Electronic Church is converting new Christians, and
that these are attaching themselves to local evangelical churches, then there will be an obvious snow-
ball effect and the hoped-for revival will soon arrive.
It will have been caused by those far-sighted
evangelical entrepreneurs who have bought their
way on to the airwaves of America.

However, on one historical fact there is com-
plete agreement. The end of the comfortable,
government-regulated arrangement with the broadcasting industry was the real kiss of death to the
mainline churches' involvement in broadcasting.
The goodwill of the networks was not enough. In
any case their goodwill was tainted by what Theo-
dore H. White, musing on his own involvement
with television, describes as irremedial schizophre-
nia. A network truly wants to operate in the public
interest. It also wants to make money.

Chapter 4

The pit and the pendulum

It is February, and unseasonably warm on America's East Coast. Only a few days earlier, the icicles had to be hacked from space shuttle *Challenger*. Eight miles above Florida, seven space heroes had met a fiery, televised death. America is heartbroken. Not since the assassinations of President Kennedy and Martin Luther King has there been national grief like this. In Washington DC, the flags hang limp at half mast in the unexpected sunshine. The President has postponed his constitutional privilege of a State of the Union address to Congress. Instead, he flies to Houston. With sincerity and republican simplicity, he quietly hugs the fatherless and the widows. The bands play *America the Beautiful*. The fireball that was *Challenger* has been played and replayed. Now, across a continent, Americans in their tens of millions look tearfully through the television lenses. They look right over the President's shoulder into the close-up faces of the bereaved.

Is this really a shared grief? Or could it just be a strange kind of entertainment? There isn't a dry eye in the house where there is a TV set. But then there never was after any showing of *Gone With the Wind* or *Bambi*. Were the space heroes real? They were real enough to their loved ones who lived with them and strove with them and held them and loved them. Are they now loved by a television audience of millions? Or have they become the stars of a short-lived two-dimensional tragedy?

Back in the nation's capital, the flags begin to climb up to full staff. In one of the expensive corners of the city, off Connecticut Avenue, the Sher-

● *Sheraton flags at half mast honour Challenger's astronauts*

aton Hotel prepares to receive an army of men and women who are dedicated to winning souls electronically and making real the love of God through television. It has to be admitted that the emotional high point of their Convention will be a wordless *Challenger* video created tastefully and very movingly for this gathering of communicators by the Christian Broadcasting Network.

NRB began life as a haven for the outcasts of broadcasting. Evangelicals were on the outside looking in. It is part of their folklore that they were excluded from network broadcasting by a cosy coalition of Catholics, mainline Protestants and Jews in the 'sweetheart deal'. But it is in the nature of secular broadcasting to deny access to a narrow and particular message. Whatever its merits, a gospel that stresses salvation for some and a Christless eternity for others can hardly be said to have a totally broad appeal.

American evangelicals continue to agonise over the separation of church and state. In a democratic situation there is no reason at all why the 'elect' of God should have special access to public broadcasting. On the other hand, the dynamics of evangelism seem to demand that every opportunity should be seized to show the way to Heaven and to divert the listener from Hell. This is the continuing dilemma of religious broadcasting. From the beginning,

Catholics and liberal Protestants were prepared to work within the agenda of the secular broadcasting industry—and, in the process, to abandon any attempt at directly proclaiming 'the gospel'. Some have seen this work as pre-evangelism and in no way a substitute for the local person-to-person church. Others see it as a shameless abdication to secularism.

The evangelicals, on the other hand, had what they considered to be the Message but they did not possess the Medium with which to broadcast it. Nowadays the medium is theirs as well—at least they believe it is. Evangelicals have their own television stations. They have cable networks and multi-million-dollar budgets. The pendulum has swung over to their side. They dominate the television screens of America; and perhaps they will soon do so across the globe. But the $64,000 question is this. Many would say religious education in schools is an improper vehicle for evangelism. Could it be that owner-operated religious television is an equally improper medium? Could it be that the old sweetheart deal in network broadcasting was in fact the best way of hinting at the love story—that God so loved the world, and that the two can co-operate?

But it has to be said that there is another side to the argument. Is the real complaint of the liberal Protestants that they simply do not like evangelicals? They do not like evangelical attitudes, nor the sermons that seem to demand oversimplified Yes and No, Heaven or Hell answers. Liberals might interpret 'conversion' as a process rather than an event. They might value the story of the flood but doubt that polar bears were aboard the Ark. They dislike an evangelical approach in a church and resent it even more so on television. But is there really any great difference between a 'talking head' in a Protestant pulpit and another on a hundred thousand TV screens? Both exemplify the now much condemned 'one way communication'. Have not the liberal communicators found in television a convenient scapegoat on which to hang all their pent-up frustration with old-time religion?

Meanwhile the irony is with so many evangelical broadcasters that, now they have the medium, they are increasingly unsure about how to deal with their message. The talk now is all of 'value-oriented material' and 'family viewing' and old but wholesome movies. 'Christian' broadcasting is coming to mean 'value-centred', 'moral', 'decent', 'American' and 'in the Judaeo-Christian tradition'. This may or may not strike blows against the American evangelicals' mythical bogeymen, the 'secular humanists', but it is certainly not *evangelical* as the term was understood by the Reformers.

There are no second thoughts in the Sheraton Hotel. National Religious Broadcasters are in town. Most of the cardinals of the Electronic Church are here but not on too public display. They have their private suites and, as befits an upper class, they mix with each other, with their monsignori and with their flunkeys. Pat Robertson is here. He is now the most important cardinal in this church without a pope. He is the Founder/President of the Christian Broadcasting Network, the biggest religious broadcasting enterprise in the world, with a nine-figure annual turnover. His has been an American dream come true, and he is introduced to one prayer breakfast as someone who 'employs four thousand people'. 'Will he or won't he?' is the well stage-managed question. He has been waiting on God to find out whether or not he should run for President. He tells the convention: 'It's time for us to say we can do better. It's only going to happen if people like you and me get involved.' Before the week is out *Robertson 88* campaign buttons will appear on many breasts; which some would hardly understand as waiting upon the Lord. This doesn't quite launch him into the Presidential role. Indeed, a premature launch would deprive him of his greatest asset, for, as a candidate, he would be obliged to remove himself from his popular *700 Club* programme on CBN.

Is the unity of the Electronic Church under strain? Another cardinal, Jerry Falwell, is here too. He was a political prelate long before Pat Robertson. He founded the Moral Majority, and he has just merged it into a new citizens' action group which he has called the Liberty Federation. Pastor Falwell has already nailed his colours to the Presidential mast and has endorsed Vice-President George Bush for the race for the White House.

As the convention gets under way, other princes of the Electronic Church appear at the top tables. Oral Roberts—now that Rex Humbard has almost gone, the doyen of the college of cardinals—is here. Evangelist Jimmy Swaggart has now supplanted Roberts in the popularity pecking order. They sit side by side at a prayer breakfast in honour of the State of Israel. Ranking at least one notch lower in this four-day consistory are the lesser luminaries, not quite cardinals, but archbishops at least, or possibly mitred abbots. David Mainse from Canada is here. He is the host of the *100 Huntley Street* programme and has an interest in broadcast evangelism in Africa and in Europe. There is Dan Betzer, of the *Revivaltime* radio programme. And over there is the personable Dr James Dobson, of *Focus On the Family*, and specialist on what every husband should know about his wife and vice versa. Billy Graham arrives to collect an NRB award for merit. President Reagan, his timetable disrupted by the *Challenger* disaster, cannot appear. Billy Graham, with the widest worldview in the whole assembly, deputises for the President and reminisces at short notice about his contacts with Communists. Could it be that this good friend of Oral Roberts is really something of a liberal in evangelical clothing? It is unlikely for, as well as being a friend of the Queen of England and Roman cardinals, he is also the author of *Till Armageddon*.

Show business is the close relation of religious broadcasting. Some would say it is the same thing. Pat Boone is announced, and Billy Graham decides his other four pressing engagements in Washington are not so pressing after all. Hollywood actor Dean Jones gives a personal testimony. And moving slowly round the crowds is the ponderous, eye-rivetting figure of the Hollywood monster man Richard (*Jaws*) Kiel. He turns out to be quiet and gentle, a born-again believer, with his own ministry in 'quality films for today's audiences'. He says fame and fortune took a toll on his life. After acquiring debt, depression and addiction to alcohol, he was 'set free' while watching 'Christian television'. Motoring smoothly among the crowds comes Joni Earackson Tada. Beautiful, and with the healthiest complexion in the whole hotel, she broke her neck after a reckless dive in the Chesapeake and has been confined ever since to a wheelchair. A quadraplegic, the gorgeous Joni speaks and sings movingly of a faith and new mobility in Christ that none could doubt.

The whole event is billed as a convention and exposition. On the second day, a set of doors in the bowels of the Sheraton slide open to reveal the religious broadcasting industry's very own trade fair. Publishers, Jews for Jesus, the Lord's Airline, and purveyors of advanced low-cost digital effects with 'zoom, flips and wipes' jostle with turnkey video-conferencing services, the Free Congress Foundation and 'Love Packages', which sounds alarming but is a 'Bible recycling centre'. Over there in the 'personality booth' stands the elegant but now rather haggard figure of the recently converted John Z. DeLorean. He's written *Deliverance*, a book about his new-found faith; and his publishers, Zondervan Books, have brought him along with five hundred free copies.

Some of the 300 stands in the inter-connecting halls beneath the Sheraton are lavish and would be a credit to the Paris Motor Show. Robert Tilton, a rising force in the Electronic Church but not yet a cardinal, has brought a TV studio from his Word of Faith World Outreach Center in Dallas. He is 'official carrier' for this NRB Convention. In 1985 he and his wife Marte 'prayerfully pulled the switch' and launched a 24-hour Success-N-Life Satellite Television Network, using the Satcom IV satellite. Pastor Tilton believes the 'whole person can have success in every area of life—spirit, mind and body—through the Lordship of Christ, by applying time-honoured and proven Biblical principles of success'. This week, his own *Success-N-Life* programme goes out from his portable studio at the Sheraton. He interviews DeLorean while the crowds gawp. Great efforts have been made with his set. Outside his very public studio is a picture of himself, dwarfed (so topically and tragically, as it turns out) by a big cut-out of a space shuttle at full throttle. Robert Tilton has a worldwide vision and 'will be in Europe soon'.

An escalator ride up from the teeming exhibition halls of the Sheraton is a relatively quiet area for lounging. A sunken area round a gentle fountain contains eight horseshoe-shaped sofas. With a non-evangelical clientele, it would be a place for scotch on the rocks and discreet transactions. During the NRB convention, the evangelicals (or rather their servants) dispense with the whisky but transact mightily. To those in the know, this well-upholstered hole in the hotel floor is known as The Pit. Those who meet there are the Pit Group—an altogether unofficial name for the most experienced and distinguished buyers of religious airtime in the entire United States. Some members of this brilliant and witty group of men and (one or two) women have grown understandably cynical after long years in the business. One of them is revered as the human being who bought most airtime .... most cheaply .... on the fewest number of stations .... with the greatest number of viewers .... in the whole of recorded history. The result of this in-spired economy is one of the great television tem-ples most certainly built with hands .... his hands. Another Pit Grouper (not himself a Christian) has mixed with the born-again for so long that all the evangelical one-liners trip naturally from his tongue. He is an academic and a raconteur. He is said to have located a veritable treasure trove of pub-lic domain (ie, out of copyright) black and white movies, which he sells to the family-conscious Christian stations and networks. In exchange he re-ceives airtime which he then sells to other agents—including the members of the Pit Group.

These are the buyers who sit at the top of their profession. Without their talent and flair, the cardinals of the Electronic Church would be reduced to the ranks—and very quickly. These people spend tens of millions of dollars to keep their masters on the screens of America. They enjoy the convention too. It is for them also a professional gathering—a chance to enjoy old cronies and forge new alliances, to exchange gossip and the latest wicked stories. Underneath them (both literally and figuratively) are hundreds of lesser buyers. These lower mortals flit around the exhibition halls giving it something of the air of a stock exchange. They dart and weave and wheel and deal and then queue for one of the Sheraton's altogether insufficient quantity of telephones to confirm their transactions with the outside world. To stand in a telephone line at the NRB convention is a frustrating, time-consuming, most unspiritual, but enlightening experience.

Throughout the hotel, in rooms and halls named after the Presidents of the United States, there are seminars and meetings for the delegates. There are Hispanic workshops, special events for black broadcasters, sessions on gospel music, the future of children's television, Christian women and contemporary technology. Then there are great plenary sessions for broadcasters in their thousands in the massive ballroom. Depending on the popularity of the seminars and lectures upstairs, the number in the lower-level exhibition areas ebbs and flows. Support for the Nicaraguan Contras is a recurring theme on many stands. So is support for America's anti-abortion movement. One exhibit even boasts a set of rather badly made and lurid plastic foetuses.

The grandest display of all belongs to the PTL Network founded by the diminutive but supercharged Jim Bakker and his wife Tammy Faye. As a television enterprise, PTL may seem to be a look-alike version of the bigger and earlier CBN Network. Indeed, Jim and Tammy Bakker used to work for Pat Robertson. But there is one great difference, and it is off-screen. It is explained clearly and confidently at this exhibition. Where Robertson and Roberts and Falwell have developed their universities, the Bakkers have created Heritage USA,

'America's most exciting family park located in the heart of the Carolinas'. Heritage USA has a new Grand Hotel with over 500 luxurious rooms. Or there is a 96-room Heritage Inn, or a choice of lakeside chalets. Even timeshare facilities are on offer. There is 'exquisite formal dining in Hampton Court' and 'scrumptious pizzas in Granny's Kitchen'. Located at the massive Heritage Grand Center is Main Street. According to the leaflet, 'From the moment you step on the cobblestone street, you'll feel you've stepped back in time. Quaint storefronts beckon shoppers to experience such delightful places as Heavenly Fudge Shop, Noah's Toy Shoppe, Goosebumps, Perry's Emporium, Aunt Susie's Ice Cream Parlor and Der Bakker Bakery'. There is a Heritage Village Church, pastored by Jim Bakker, an Upper Room and even an Easter Passion Play. Also, of course, there are ultra-modern television studios and satellite facilities. There is a Heritage School of Evangelism and Communication and a People That Love Opportunity Farm for Homeless Men.

One of the liberal Christian's criticisms of the Electronic Church is that the televangelists cannot effect person-to-person contact. This may well be true of the television programmes; but the spin-off ministries—Bakker's Heritage enterprises, Schuller's Cathedral, Oral Roberts' gigantic facility in Tulsa—certainly touch many thousands of people.

Ninety-nine per cent of the delegates to this convention would not call themselves mainline Christians. A lone Episcopalian stands sentry guard over a small stall advertising Anglican prayer. Father John Bertolucci, a charismatic Catholic who preaches like a Protestant revivalist, is highly visible at the Sheraton, and is well received. 'It is possible to be a Catholic and a Christian,' someone whispers charitably. There are a few West Europeans. Great sympathy is extended to these persecuted broadcasters, downtrodden by their state broadcasting monopolies and prevented from preaching the Gospel. But they are not to worry. Help is on the way. Satellites—God's angels in the sky, and foretold in the Book of Revelation—will soon be beaming *The Hour of Power* and *The 700 Club* to Europe's spiritually starving masses. This will occur whether the European governments want it to do so or not. 'Come over to Macedonia and help us' is the gist of what the handful of Old World broadcasters are saying in the Sheraton Hotel. A kind of spiritual Marshall Aid will soon be bouncing off the satellites to erode the twin enemies of religious unbelief and 'Socialist', governmental control of what should be a free-market broadcasting system.

National Religious Broadcasters is not a movement of nearly identical minds. It is first and foremost a trade association for a religious broadcasting industry managed by those who would come under the broad title of evangelical. NRB has its own codes of ethics and financial accountability. It has special life insurance schemes for its members and the beginnings of an employment placement service. If NRB did not already exist, it would certainly need to be invented; for religious broadcasting in the United States is now under-pinned by a unique economic system that stands quite apart from the rest of American broadcasting. 'Back-to-back' religious programming is set up to appeal to a donor base. In the strict sense of the word, it is no longer broadcasting. It is targetted to a distinct group who will provide the finance for future broadcasts. It is hoped, of course, that all kinds of viewers will appreciate the output, but it is expected that one category of viewer will pick up the bill. The Parable of the Sower is still the inspiration. The seed is being broadcast as never before. But out there among the furrows, between the tares and the stony ground, are some special tender shoots whose green leaves are dollar bills which they send up to the Sower to keep him working.

The executive director of NRB is Dr Ben Armstrong. A kindly and self-effacing man among so many prima donnas, he presides over a permanent staff and secretariat. First impression are of a rather Dickensian, quill-pen character. The visitor to his offices in Parsippany, New Jersey, might be for-

• *NRB Director Ben Armstrong*

given for wondering if Armstrong created NRB or NRB created Armstrong. But this rather threadbare image is entirely deceptive. When animated, he looks and sounds like a lively New Yorker. The wood-panelled walls of his office are covered with photographs of his encounters with successive Presidents.

In the Electronic Church as a whole, higher academic degrees are two a penny or even cheaper. Dr Armstrong is the real thing. He has a PhD in Communication from New York University, where his specialities were Moscow Radio and Izvestia. He is a graduate of the liberal Union Theological Seminary and an ordained minister of the Presbyterian Church USA. For eight years he was director of radio with the Monte Carlo-based Trans World Radio. He has an attractive blonde wife and the best sense of humour in the Sheraton. His book *The Electric Church* gives a more than comprehensive but quite uncritical survey of the history and scope of broadcast religion. More than any man alive, Ben Armstrong knows the ins and outs of the Electronic Church. From Archbishop Sheen to Robert Schuller and Oral Roberts, he has known them all, and written about them all, and they are all fine by him. As someone else once said, 'all have won and all shall have prizes'.

But of course this hotel is not just full of the great and the glorious. Most of the big stars are upstairs in their suites or jetting hither and thither, and only making occasional scheduled appearances among the lesser mortals. Most of the broadcasters here will never make it to the big time. Most of them are motivated and idealistic. Dr Paul Broyles used to be a highly paid corporate lawyer with an oil company. He changed direction to found the International Broadcasting Network in Houston. From a two-station Texas base, he plans to reach out with the gospel to other countries. From his days in oil, he knows what it is like to be a Christian under an alien religious regime. He is also highly sensitive to the dangers of exporting American culture. Broyles has made obvious and considerable sacrifices for his evangelistic convictions. He says of his work, 'I do not view it in any sense as a *business* but of course try to operate on a sound and prudent basis'.

Will the biggest name of all be at this year's convention? President Reagan usually comes; but it is said that last year he tried to make excuses. According to the gossip, a message went across the city to the White House and said: 'You had better come because these are the people who elected you.' No. This year he cannot come; but with good reason. The *Challenger* disaster has meant that both he and the Vice-President must reschedule their arrangements. Instead there is a Presidential greeting on video. True, the President's message does mention 'Our Lord' and denounces abortion. But it is mainly a political and foreign policy manifesto. No doubt the script writers are occupied with the State of the Union Address that will be delivered later in the week.

This convention is not afraid of politics. Courtesy of an incompetent computer, Senator Edward Kennedy became enrolled in the Moral Majority. He declined to pay his dues but offered instead to debate Jerry Falwell. This heroic joust took place before the assembled knights of the previous year's NRB Convention. This year's clay pigeon is former Congressman John Buchanan, of People for the American Way, a political organisation founded by television producer Norman Lear, which works to preserve the separation of church and state as guaranteed by the First Amendment. 'You will never arrive at a situation of grace through government fear,' says Dr Buchanan, himself a Southern Baptist minister. The champion for the evangelical army is evangelist Jimmy Swaggart. He looks back to the Revolutionary War and to leaders who invoked the help of God: 'They said, God, if you will help us, we will give this country to you.'

And so this very stately battle rolls along. But to the evangelicals it is an all-important battle. Is America a Christian country (or at least a Godly country), or is it not? Does 'the law of God' on issues like abortion and school prayers take precedence over the law of the United States? It follows, too, that if America does indeed belong to God, the nation's broadcasting should have the same proprietor. Evangelicals seem to have forgotten Thomas Jefferson. They believe that if they can roll back secularism they will reveal a purer, original version of America.

But the heady mix of politics and religion that is filling the Sheraton Hotel is not all about the American Constitution. In recent years there has grown up an alliance between evangelicals and Zionists. These two American groups, who would seem by any standards to be at odds with one another, have become allies. The noisiest Christians—the ones who are possibly most uncompromising about the literal claims of the New Testament—have become bedfellows with those who reject the divinity of Christ. There are all kinds of reasons why this dizzy romance is unlikely to mature into a true marriage. The preservation of the State of Israel is not a gut preoccupation of groups like the Moral Majority (now subsumed into the Liberty Federation). American Jewry has yet to be dislodged from the American liberal camp.

On the Jewish side of the new 'alliance' it is not difficult to discern strictly utilitarian reasons for obtaining as many friends as possible. Israel still needs every ally it can get. Any sign that anti-semitism is breaking down is to be welcomed. Some rabbis see the overtures from the evangelicals as 'acceptance' of Judaism and as the beginning of the end of a proselytising Christianity. One Jewish observer in the Sheraton Hotel quotes her father, a rabbi: 'You know, if we try hard enough we can make them hate us. They've done it for centuries.'

On the evangelical Christian side of the fence there have been developments in recent years. Most of these changes have come from a re-emphasis on biblical prophecy. The end is believed to be near. These are the 'end times'. God still has a purpose for his ancient people the Jews. The re-establishment of the State of Israel is interpreted as a sign that the time is short and that God's plans for

• *Sounds of joy at the Sheraton*

this world are nearing a conclusion. Hence the Fifth National Prayer Breakfast in Honor of Israel.

Here in the Sheraton, as the NRB convention nears its end, religious broadcasters and rabbis and national politicians meet to cement this alliance of opposites. Elsewhere in the building the Black Religious Broadcasters are also breaking their fast. Their guest of honour is Jesse Jackson, and their breakfast is an official part of the convention programme. It is a flop. Only 125 people turn up. Black leaders, humiliated and embarrassed by the small turnout, blame the NRB organisers and the magnetism of Israel. Ben Armstrong, ever the optimist, is unabashed. He says 125 black broadcasters is the biggest number there has ever been. He rates the black breakfast a success.

The early morning encounter with Israel really is a success. The Sheraton's Cotillion Room is crowded. Pat Robertson is looking and behaving as a President should. Jimmy Swaggart, Oral Roberts, David Mainse and Mrs Armstrong are joined by Senator Albert Gore and a clutch of Congressmen. Rabbis David Ben-Ami, Alex Pollack and Joshua

O.Haberman represent the Old Covenant. Miss National Teenager is here too, for no particular reason except that she is very pretty. Father Bertolucci's Roman collar looks eccentric. He is introduced as the man 'whose preaching will knock the socks off you', which he seems to take as a compliment. The Likud Party is represented, and so are the White House, the Lord's Airline and Israeli Tourism. The talk at the tables is of the Second Coming, or at least Armageddon. To warm applause from everyone, the attache from the embassy urges a holiday in Israel next summer.

Ben Armstrong seems preoccupied. He is announced several times, but his seat on the top table is empty. Perhaps he is pacifying the under-supported black broadcasters in the other room. Speaker after speaker extols the rapprochement between the Jewish and evangelical communities. To loud laughter and not a few 'Amens' Colonel Gaddafi is described as the 'real Mediterranean fruit-fly'. The last minutes of the human era are ticking away. In the next five years we are going to see the hand of God moving in the Holy Land as never before. Could Armageddon be that near? All this is too much for a portly Greek-Australian newsman, who says 'Blotty Americans' in a loud voice, fortunately drowned by a solo rendering of the Battle Hymn of the Republic.

Pat Robertson speaks of Israeli Premiers he has known. He himself has suffered commercially from Middle East violence. His TV station in Jordan was car-bombed twice at a cost of $500,000. The Greek-Australian representative of the Fourth Estate is amused by this disclosure. Dr Pat is going to 'blanket Syria with a city-grade signal'. He refers to the 'so-called West Bank'; he wants the United States to acknowledge Jerusalem as Israel's capital. He condemns Britain for selling high-performance fighters to Israel's enemies. He thinks socialism is a failed ideology.

The keynote speaker is Jeane Kirkpatrick. In her deep and languid drawl, a Yankee transposition of Marlene Dietrich, she puts Pat Robertson to rights on two specifics and then itemises, in fine scholarly detail, ten good reasons why the United States should support Israel. Her speech is not even slightly religious but entirely geo-political, as befits an ex-permanent representative to the United Nations. But she does, right at the end, stumble, as if by accident, across a vaguely theological expression, 'Judaeo-Christian values'. There is warm applause from Jewry and 'Amen' and 'Hallelujah' from Christendom. 'That dame's too smart for the Americans,' says the Greek-Australian, puffing cigarette smoke over a small congregation of charismatics.

Breakfast concludes with prayer, broadcaster style. Evangelist Jimmy Swaggart and four lesser lights take it in turns to pray for the peace of Jerusalem. God has a purpose still for the 'Root' as well as the 'Branch'. 'Amens' and 'Hallelujahs' resound from every breakfast table. The rabbis look at the ceiling, one of them—clearly a man of faith—walking round the Cotillion Room while he does so. The Greek-Australian is finally defeated by this quite unreportable Judaeo-Christian experience and beats a noisy retreat from the room. Dr Ben Armstrong is in his seat at last—or is he? More 'Amens'. More 'Hallelujahs'. The Christian broadcasters are praying harder. Some of the Children of Israel are talking quietly among themselves. Silence at last. Everyone stands for the National Anthem—of Israel.

Chapter 5

Angels in the sky

It was Dr Ben Armstrong who first coined the phrase Electric Church. Most people now prefer to be more up to date and call it the Electronic Church. Both are useful shorthand expressions, and both are used by supporters and opponents alike. But the very use of an umbrella term like Electronic Church implies a unity of purpose and theology that does not in fact exist. There is only one great uniting factor, and that is the financial basis for the whole 'church'. The evangelistic associations and the Christian networks all buy their time. There is only one way to avoid buying airtime, and that is to buy the whole station. The Electronic Church is firmly united by the realities of the marketplace. Time-buying has to come before anything else. NRB is first and foremost a trade association.

Clearly, the electronic evangelists have to be successful businessmen. They believe there is no conflict of conscience between religion and a free enterprise system. Far from it. God calls religious broadcasting into a business of ministry and, so long as business principles are upright, he will use commercial success as a 'testimony for his honour and glory'. Obviously, as businessmen in a large but nevertheless limited marketplace, the evangelists are in competition with each other. The mark of success is to have enough dollars available ... to buy enough time ... to ensure enough exposure ... to attract enough dollars ... to buy enough time ... to ensure enough exposure ... Competition between the various evangelistic units is not scandalously fierce. Like any industry there are friendships and links at many levels. Accountants, cameramen and administrators often move on to work for another evangelist. There are commercial and ideological alliances, cemented in at least one case by an honorary doctorate. The success of one preacher can mean the decline and fall of another. Jimmy Swaggart and Jerry Falwell are near the top of the financial tree, while the empire of the ageing Oral Roberts is under some strain. Collectively, the televangelists are not so much an Electronic Church but rather a group of Christian businessmen.

● *Billy Graham: enthusiastic about the Electronic Church*

Unsurprisingly, the Electronic Church includes the good, the great and the gentle as well as the downright dishonest and the bizarre. Sadly there is no process of selectivity which can sort out the good, the bad and the indifferent. The mainline churches tend to dismiss the whole business—as a business. People on the evangelical side of the fence who should know better refuse to be discriminating. They approve of the Electronic Church—all of it and without reservation. Billy Graham is enthusiastic, despite hearing widespread remarks about the Sunday morning religious ghetto. He watches the programmes and thanks God for them and what they have been able to do. This is not simply a public stance but comes from a widely held but nevertheless naive optimism. 'Okay, it's true,' admits the marketing director for one of the Christian networks. 'There is some junk out there alongside all the good material. But God can use and sanctify even that junk. He can make use of anything.'

A number of the preachers, particularly those at local level who represent strong local churches, would be happy to be called evangelical, or perhaps conservative evangelical, to emphasise their attitude to scripture. Some preachers would want to go further and stand absolutely four-square on the literal interpretation of the Bible. With Jerry Falwell, they would be happy to be known as fundamentalists. Others—and this is now the most visible group on big-time religious broadcasting—would call themselves charismatics.

Fundamentalist and charismatic mean different things to different people. There is no tidily-fenced fundamentalist movement and no charismatic church. There is a formula which some use to explain the difference: 'All charismatics are fundamentalists but not all fundamentalists are charismatics.' But this is too neat and does not take account of the influential American Catholic Charismatics, who are certainly not fundamentalists. A fundamentalist looks to the Bible. Charismatics emphasise the here-and-now experience of the living Holy Spirit. In many local situations in the United States there is no love lost between the two.

To make matters even more confusing, there are three broad strands of belief concerning the end of the world; and all three are found in both the fundamentalist and the charismatic camps. Millennialists believe that Christ will return in person and institute a thousand-year reign in Jerusalem, and then will come the end. Amillennialists expect Christ's return and the end of the world to occur at the same time. Postmillennialists believe the millennium will be followed by the Second Coming. Overlaying these different expectations are various beliefs about the so-called Rapture, the hope that some true believers will not in fact die but be caught up in the air with Christ.

Most of these beliefs come from a literal interpretation of the Book of Revelation. Among the vast majority of American Christians, the Roman Catholics, the mainline churches and even some Baptist churches, there is a conviction that time will come to an end and that each human being will one day give account to God. There is a generally held belief that somehow all things will come together for good with God, but no details. Even the Catholic belief in purgatory is fading.

On the other hand, fundamentalists and particularly charismatics provide a variety of blow-by-blow accounts of the 'end times'. A number of highly detailed forecasts have proved to be bestsellers. They are crammed with interesting speculations. The consensus seems to be that the USA is likely to decline; the European Common Market will become the nucleus of a one-world government. In order to fulfill the biblical plan, the Common Market will have to consist of just ten nations. Perhaps Britain and one other will be expelled. There will come one who will provide political leadership and appear to be a peacemaker among all the nations with the good of Europe at heart. He will be the Antichrist. During the fifth stage of the war of Armageddon, the Antichrist will be in Israel and he will be under attack from a 200 million-man army from the Orient.

Over two million copies of *There's a New World Coming*, Hal Lindsey's 'in depth' analysis of the Book of Revelation, are in print. It has been warmly welcomed by some of the charismatic televangelists. Trinity Broadcasting Network distributed its own special edition, including a back-cover portrait of Paul and Jan Crouch.

Charismatic influence is very strong in the Electronic Church. Among those who would call themselves charismatics are Jimmy Swaggart and Oral Roberts. The three best-known Christian TV networks, CBN, PTL and the Crouches' TBN are managed by Spirit-filled believers.

There is an intense preoccupation with the end of the world. The re-establishment of the State of Israel is seen as the fulfilment of biblical prophecy. God still has a detailed plan for the people of Israel and especially for the 144,000 Jewish evangelists mentioned in Revelation. Not all the charismatic preachers would go down a meticulously detailed road and predict an army making a banzai charge through the dried-up bed of the River Euphrates. All, however, talk of 'these end times'. Several retain reporters in Jerusalem, which is where the action is going to be. Time is ticking away in what televangelists call 'the countdown'.

Between the mainline churches and evangelicals generally there is a disagreement over the meaning of prophecy. Evangelicals believe that the Prophets could look into the future, and that the books of Daniel and Revelation in particular are a kind of miraculous crystal ball vision of what is to come; a divinely inspired glimpse into the future. In the liberal, mainline camp, this interpretation is out of favour. Prophecy is seen as inspired interpretation of the signs of the times. What about the many prophetic passages linking Old and New Testaments? How can a prophecy such as the Isaiah passage about the birth of a child not refer to Jesus? Some mainline scholars would claim that rather than Old Testament writers enjoying a glimpse across the centuries, New Testament writers searched the Old Testament for 'prophecies' to support their narrative.

In the Electronic Church, there is no place for subtleties. A prophecy is nothing if it is not a miraculous preview of what is to come. The electronic evangelists even see themselves in the Bible.

There is a famous story of when David Du Plessis, the Pentecostal leader, met Karl Barth. Barth was sceptical of Bible predictions about the future and asked why radio and television were not mentioned in scripture. 'Oh, they are,' said Du Plessis, and told the Swiss theologian to look up Revelation 14:6. This passage says: 'And I saw another Angel flying in the midst of heaven, having the everlasting Gospel to preach unto them that dwell on the earth.' Some evangelicals and large numbers of charismatics believe that the 'Angel' is in fact a broadcast satellite.

The Dominion Network, committed to direct religious broadcast by satellite and thus bypassing local broadcast and cable systems, has produced a record with singer Evie Karlsson about its plans for a two-winged angel in orbit, which incidentally would be 30 times more powerful than the first-generation broadcast satellites.

It was in the 1980s
At the end of Ages
I saw the people on the Earth
The turmoil, fear and doubt
I could hear the children crying
And see the world was dying
In sin and darkness and oppression
By the evil one.

Then I saw another angel in the sky
Proclaiming the eternal gospel
Saying in another voice
Fear God and give him glory
For the time has come for his judgement.

To most American Christians it is incredible to suggest that St John, writing down his apocalyptic visions on the island of Patmos nearly two thousand years ago, could in fact have been shown something like a Hughes Aircraft Company HS 394 communications satellite. Separated from the mainline churches by a grand canyon when it comes to the meaning of scripture, evangelicals can at least admit the possibility of solar-powered aluminium angels with 24 transponders!

Unfortunately St John was not really specific about the future. The usual explanation for this is that visions into the twentieth century would have overtaxed the descriptive powers and the vocabulary of a first-century writer. There is one passage which describes a locust with the face of a man, the teeth of a lion, a breastplate of iron, a tail that can sting, and wings that make the sound of many chariots. The Apostle would be at a loss for words to describe what might be a very modern helicopter.

Whether they believe these shiny mechanisms are angels or not, America's evangelical broadcasters certainly welcome satellites just as they welcomed radio and television. They believe that with a growing world population and with the end approaching, there is only one way to fulfil Christ's commission to preach the Gospel to all the nations, and that is by utilising the latest broadcasting technology. These urgent evangelists are also American patriots. They share with the nation as a whole a deep pride in America's space achievements.

Many of the space heroes are Christians. When Soviet Cosmonaut Gagarin entered the heavens he 'couldn't see God'. American Astronaut Bormann, on the other hand, in orbit round the Moon, was moved to recite: 'In the beginning, God created the heaven and the earth.' Commander James Irwin, of Moon Buggy fame, speaks movingly of his first view of Earth from the surface of the Moon. 'I felt like an angel,' he says. He now has his own evangelistic outreach ministry encouraging 'high flight' with Jesus. The Mormons, too, have their own space-man, Dr Don Lind.

Space and religion are a powerful mixture. The once wild West is now full of highways and cafeterias. The new frontier is on the way to the stars. The spirit of Columbus lives again with the astronauts. Industry has new worlds to conquer. The nation's armed forces are preparing to defend America from space. Cosmologists are looking out into the galaxy for an understanding of both our origin and destiny. To a nation brought up on the morality plays of science fiction, space speaks of God and of science and of the American spirit.

Paradoxically, space makes a much better cock-tail when mixed with the certainties of fundamentalism than with the ifs and buts of liberal Christianity. It is a strange marriage in many ways, but the mainline churches were not suitors. They pride themselves on a stronger commitment to the human problems of Planet Earth and have been less impressed with the high cost of space travel. The fundamentalists have no regard for 'creationist nonsense', but they are not opposed to science and technology. Far from it. Many of the TV preachers cultivate a hi-tech image. Oral Roberts's newest attraction in Tulsa will be a special audio visual presentation of the Bible starting with the Genesis creation story and using 'space technology'.

Satellite uplink dishes are wonderfully large, potent symbols. They are the totem poles of the Electronic Church. In previous centuries, madonnas and crucifixes were the outward and visible signs. Now satellite dishes have become the spires for go-ahead Christians. They represent a communicating, up-to-date Church that is addressing the whole nation. Americans in general are not yet blasé about their satellites. 'Satellite TV' is still a plus for a motel anywhere in the country. The receiver dish is rarely hidden away but sometimes even floodlit in the car park to advertise a caring, modern manage-

• *Potent symbol: a satellite uplink dish*

ment. So it is with the studios of the Electronic Church. In the new post-print age, the Word of God can be fired out of huge uplink gospel megaphones.

The drawback, of course, is that mass communication kills two-way communication. Big dishes may have improved sermons but they have obliterated sacraments. Huge status symbols like Paul Crouch's Holy Beamer speak to the world but listen to no-one. A few of the Evangelists are aware of the problem. The search is on for communion as well as for communication, for an inter-active Electronic Church.

At present, the public—even the believing public—can only access each evangelist's computer and word processor. These machines do not reply with mere pro-forma letters. Hundreds of the preacher's phrases, anecdotes, expressions and even innermost convictions are stored on the computer's software. Each reply is 'personalised', and probably resembles the kind of caring and specific reply that the evangelist would have written if he had had the time. But the fact remains that he did not write the letter, that he does not know 'Dear Ruth' or 'Dear Ed'. The only personal contact open to the viewer is by telephone to one of the large team of volunteers who process donations and prayer requests. The telephonist-Christians are motivated and usually well-trained counsellors; but they are not the man himself.

As the name implies, the Electronic Church owes everything to computers, word processors and telephone banks—and to the satellites, the 'birds' that have themselves revolutionised American broadcasting. The satellite is in fact an electronic relay station powered by solar panels. The early moving satellites had to be tracked from the ground, and communication was possible only at certain times. Nowadays it is possible to establish a geosynchronous orbit. As the earth rotates, each satellite travels at the same speed as the planet's rotation and remains over a particular part of the surface. In other words, these birds do not fly. They hang in fixed positions over the earth, acting as electronic mirrors. Radio waves are first cousins to light waves and behave in almost the same way. The huge uplink dish is a kind of searchlight, focusing its spot beam of signals onto a satellite, which in turn converts the spotlight into a floodlight which shines back to earth and can illuminate a continent.

The United States has more than 20 broadcast satellites parked in its own internationally agreed belt over the equator. They have a lifespan of about 10 years. If a saboteur wanted to paralyse American cable television, he would not need to shoot down all 20 satellites. Two would be enough. RCA's Satcom IIIR and Hughes' Galaxy 1 are the most expensive to lease, but feed most cable systems.

The great advantage of satellite broadcasting is its efficiency. A broadcaster in San Diego can bounce a signal to a cable operator in Manhattan. This 'one-hop microwave' travels 70,000 kilometres in one fifth of a second; and of course there does not have to be just one waiting cable operator. CBN, the Christian network, using both Satcom IIIR and Galaxy 17, feeds no fewer than 5,300 cable systems. The typical satellite can carry 24 separate television channels, or even more audio channels. By leasing one of the satellite's transponders, a broadcaster can in theory reach every TV set that is cabled to every downlink within the satellite's 'footprint'. In real life, however, the audience size will depend on the size of the broadcaster's pocket book. He will have to pay the cable systems to take his programme. His final hurdle will be persuading the viewer to stay with him rather than any of the other 13 or 30 programmes on offer from the cable company.

When Winston Churchill died in 1965, CBS chartered a plane and equipped it as a mobile transatlantic editing studio, so that the state funeral could be seen by Americans in the shortest possible time. The angels in the sky have now made television international and almost instantaneous. Money is all that is needed to connect Jerusalem with New Jersey, or to put an evangelist from Baton Rouge onto a South American TV set. Within the borders of the United States, every religious broadcaster has become a national broadcaster—potentially at least.

Only a very few years ago, programme distribution was a major handicap for the big-time televangelists. In the studio complexes, there still stand huge motorised shelving systems for processing tapes. Without satellites, the Christian Broadcasting Network would have to use landlines or over-the-air links or (impossible thought) produce 5,000 separate video tapes—or produce fewer and then 'bicycle' them from station to station. Now, thanks to space shuttles and Ariane rockets, a newer wireless age has begun. Relay stations in the sky feed the programmes to America's radio and television stations and to the cable systems.

Satellites have given the electronic evangelists a new lease of life. They can speak the new language of Gigahertz and Look Angles and Footprints. God has given them a new, more powerful means of doing what they began to do in the early days of radio. He will soon give them even more powerful tools for their preaching trade. Before long, satellite broadcasting will reach the whole planet, and signals from a new breed of high-powered satellites will be able to be received by individuals using tiny dishes.

Communications technology is changing all the time, and inevitably there is some confusion in the broadcasting industry. Satellites send out a plethora of signals on different frequencies and with different polarization formats. There is disagreement over the rights and wrongs of encryption. However, before very long, home viewers will possess a new generation of 'smart' receivers capable of aligning themselves onto a selected satellite and adjusting automatically for frequency, polarization, decoding and stereo sound. Further on, the home receiver will be able to talk to its owner through a voice synthesiser and give a spoken preview of the coming week's programme highlights.

The mainline American churches have been largely unappreciative of all this angelic apparatus. Insofar as they are involved in public broadcasting, they are of course involved with satellites. But, with a few exceptions that will be dealt with in detail in a later chapter, the traditional churches have kept themselves resolutely on terra firma.

Like all big American institutions, the traditional churches have not been so slow to appreciate the *internal* benefits of satellite technology. CTNA— the Catholic Telecommunications Network of America—leases 15 hours a week on the Westar IV satellite to distribute audio and video material to 70 of the country's 170 dioceses. The weekly programming schedule includes the Mass in English and another in Spanish. There is a *Christian Lifestyle* magazine and *Maryknoll World* from the liberation-minded Maryknoll Fathers. Each receiving diocese makes its own decision about how it will handle this mixture of entertainment and educational and liturgical material. CTNA's signal is not available to the general public. It is encrypted; and decoding equipment is required at each diocesan downlink, from where material is redistributed to hospitals, schools, churches and, in some cases, cable systems.

The Southern Baptists have their own Baptist Telecommunications Network. Programming is not intended for the general public. As with the Catholic network, the BTN signal is encrypted, and is available only to some 300 Southern Baptist locations via TVRO earth stations. The network is managed by the Southern Baptist Sunday School Board. Programming is transmitted from Nashville to the Westar IV satellite and consists of Sunday School preparation, church staff training and Bible studies. Plans are being made for a church teletext service and seminary correspondence courses.

The smaller denominations will no doubt follow the Catholic and Southern Baptist examples. In the Episcopal Church, a Task Force on Satellite Communication reported to the Presiding Bishop in April 1985. The report concluded that 'the question is not so much whether, but why and when. It is reasonable to predict that within the next 15 years it will be good stewardship to use a satellite transponder on a regular basis'.

The angels in the sky can be used in several quite different ways. The televangelists beam their gospel into the world of general entertainment broadcasting. The churches, on the other hand, use satellite technology for the less glamorous task of internal communication and training. There are now signs of a coming together of these two approaches. Some evangelists are praying for the new direct broadcast satellites that could by-pass the companies and provide 'faith-sustaining TV' for 'Christian homes'. Praying is only part of the answer. Paying for DBS may prove more difficult.

From his Word of Faith Outreach Center in Dallas, Pastor Robert Tilton has an extensive broadcasting ministry; but he is also heavily involved in preaching to the converted. His Sunday morning worship with his 8,000-member congregation is shared by satellite with 1,400 like-minded congregations and centres. Further programming includes Bible study, family issues, personal finances, nutrition and fitness. Members of Pastor Tilton's outreach team provide a follow-up service to the subscribing congregations and pastors.

They may have different approaches to satellite broadcasting; but in both the mainline and the electronic churches, less expensive closed-circuit television by satellite is taking off.

But even the glossiest of electronic churchmen convey a boyish and rather touching delight in their brand-new hardware. There is one wicked, and hopefully apocryphal, story in circulation. ABC's star newsman Ted Koppel often conducts lively interviews while staring at a large screen made of green felt. There is nothing on the screen, only felt: it is a device to enhance picture quality. Engineers superimpose the far-away talking head. As far as the viewer is concerned, there is no green felt screen but only a face. This is clever—real satellite television. And, so the story goes, one of the Christian networks, not to be outdone by Mr Koppel, employed the green-screen technique to interview a guest who was sitting not a thousand miles away but in the same studio.

Chapter 6

Mission impossible

Even the TV preachers have their funny stories about going through the Pearly Gates. One heavenly tale concerns Billy Graham and Oral Roberts. They both reach the after life at the same moment. Billy Graham immediately begins a preaching crusade to make sure everyone is converted. Oral Roberts checks the air-conditioning.

Oral Roberts is a builder; and the city he has built on the outskirts of Tulsa, Oklahoma, is one of the world's greatest personal acts of religious self-expression. The central themes of the Roberts ministry are carved out in concrete, glass, steel and copper. Every building on the huge campus is a sermon in stone; and the sermon is unmistakably by Oral Roberts.

There is the River of Life. It does not look much like a river but more like an ornamental canal bounded by a rather unsubtle rope of carefully plaited walls. The 'river' flows for 770 feet into an enormous arch made up of two Dürer-like healing hands. But, large though it is, this great prayer symbol is dwarfed by the three gleaming towers of the City of Faith Medical and Research Center.

Roberts thinks of everything. Tourists and honest inquirers do not, in person, have to disturb the sick in the City of Faith. On the first floor there is a special theatre containing a purpose-built audio-visual display. A battery of projectors is linked to a squad of lifesized doctors and nurses. After 20 minutes with this impressive talking waxworks, the Oral Roberts approach to health and religion has been explained.

He has the somewhat disconcerting habit of talking about himself in the third person. 'God has raised up Oral Roberts,' he says. Apart from this egocentricity, his healing message is straightforward. God heals in various ways, by direct spiritual intervention as well as through the medical profession. In the City of Faith there is a place for both prayer and medicine.

Patients occupy individual architect-designed rooms. There is a full range of medical services, and brown-uniformed prayer partners are nearby at all times. Medical and surgical staff also pray with their patients. The Roberts touch is everywhere. He has insisted on hot food staying hot and cold food staying cold—even when it is served on the same tray. Special catering equipment has been installed to solve the problem. His attention to detail extends even to the dreaded hospital gown. Backless nightshirts, the scourge of so many patients worldwide, are no more in the City of Faith.

In its three mighty towers, the healing centre has facilities for medical research and training, as well as for patient care. Critics in Oklahoma say the hospital is badly under-used. If the City of Faith turns out to be a white elephant, it will be one of the biggest failures in medical history. On the other hand, it can also be seen as perhaps the largest-scale attempt in any country to return to a New Testament standard of healing, with preaching, prayer and medicine playing a part.

Like him or loathe him, the City of Faith Health Care Center is Oral Roberts's monument. From his early tent meetings to his present eminence as ruler of his Oklahoma city-state, his has been a message of healing. 'God loves you and so do I,' smiles Robert Schuller from California. The Tulsa gospel is 'God wants you healed and so do I'.

Roberts says he and his son Richard use two different 'delivery systems' for bringing the healing power of God to hurting people. Oral uses his hands to represent 'the healing hands of Jesus'. Richard, on the other hand, 'feels the anointing in his chest and in his voice to speak out specific words of knowledge from the Lord about something God is doing in someone's life at that very moment'.

Using radio and television, Oral Roberts and Son reach out from Tulsa to those who need healing. 'If I could,' says Roberts Senior; 'if I could, and you wanted me to do it—and thousand of people do want me to do it—I would come to your house. I would lay my hands on you. I'd touch you with my right hand because I feel the presence of God in it, and I'd ask Christ to heal you. If you were taking medicine, I'd pray for God to make the medicine work better. If you were in surgery, I'd be praying to God that surgery would work. Or if I were just there to pray for you and you wanted me to—and a lot of people do—I'd lay my hands on you. I would do it. I can't come to everybody's house; but do you know, if I could I'd walk right over there where you are, and I'd hold out my right hand if you said "Oral Roberts, lay hands on me and pray for me". I'd lay my hand on you and pray for you. And those of you who believe in my ministry know I would do it. Some of you have had my hands laid upon you as you've come to our crusades and other places. I cannot come in the flesh to everyone of you anymore than Paul could.'

The problem facing all religious broadcasters is how to take the pulpit into the living rooms of America. Oral Roberts has set himself an impossible task of translating for the mass media the essentially inter-personal, flesh and blood ministry of spiritual healing. A 'Radio Doctor' programme would be easy enough, with plenty of helpful hints about healthy living. Healing, however, by its very nature cannot be a general activity. It demands personal attention and even touch. But Roberts is nothing if not an innovator, and he employs techniques that many would consider quite shocking.

According to his ex-daughter-in-law Patti, Oral Roberts has a good intellect and is widely read. On his *Expect a Miracle* programme he can sound almost like Soren Kierkegaard. 'We're going to attempt to bring the living Jesus with his divine life into your being in the now of your existence,' declaims Roberts. But the free offer that follows owes precious little to existential Christianity. 'First,' he continues, 'I want to mention this very special handerkerchief that I had made—a beautiful light blue—and printed on it EXPECT A NEW MIRA- CLE EVERY DAY.' Roberts describes his special handkerchief as a 'prayer cloth' and a 'point of con- tact'. Thousands of people have written in asking for one. It is free for the asking to the viewer or listener. And, promises Roberts, before putting it in the envelope and mailing it he will extend his right hand over it.

As a scriptural justification for sending out each 'prayer cloth', Roberts quotes the Acts of the Apos- tles. In chapter 19, verse 12, handkerchiefs and aprons (probably workmen's aprons) which had touched St Paul were taken to the sick and they were cured of their illnesses. This passage bristles with difficulties. A literal translation would read: 'so that there were even brought away from his skin handkerchiefs or aprons onto those who ailed and the diseases were rid from them'. It is not at all clear from the Greek text whether St Paul realised that cloths had been taken away from him by his zealous new converts. He would surely have discouraged such magical cures. They stand in stark contrast to the Pauline teaching on faith. There is the obvious parallel with the one who was cured by touching the hem of Christ's garment; and in this case the ini- tiative was with the sufferer rather than with the healer.

But Oral Roberts doesn't waste time on seman- tics. His interpretation of Acts 19 is a wild one, but he puts down any opposition to his own idiosyn- crasy by appealing back to the Bible. 'Of course, all Scripture's controversial with the Devil and with the Devil's crowd, and you must not allow the con- troversy *they* bring around the Word of God to dis- courage you and your healing.'

Dr Ben Armstrong writes of Oral Roberts that 'his special genius appears to be in making hope real and God close'. The prayer cloths may be intended to do just that; but the whole concept, even to many evangelicals, is dangerously bizarre. Roberts is careful to point out that the handkerchiefs are without charge; but this is not good enough. Money is solicited during *Expect a Miracle* and he lays himself wide open to a host of ethical and theological criticisms.

Prayer cloths that have been placed near Oral Roberts's supposedly significant right hand would have enraged that great Paulinist Martin Luther. He would have railed against them along with relics and other Romish practices. Pope Leo X once tried to buy off Luther's protector, Frederick of Saxony, with the coveted gift of a papal golden rose. 'Dearly beloved,' wrote His Holiness, 'the most holy golden rose was consecrated by us on the fourteenth day of the holy fast. It was anointed with holy oil and sprinkled with fragrant incense with the papal benediction.' One of the causes of the Reformation was that 'making hope real' can be taken much too far.

Nevertheless what was said of Sir Christopher Wren can be said of Oral Roberts, too: 'If you would see his monument, look about you.' Your best view will be from the City of Faith Health Care Center. All the Roberts buildings are futuristic, with a dash of Montezuma. Indeed, the whole area could well be used as the set for a science fiction epic. The Prayer Tower, where teams of telephonists are on duty 24 hours a day, resembles a flying saucer. The central column that holds it aloft gives it the look of a child's spinning top—an enormous 200-foot toy. Available in the Prayer Tower is *Journey Into Faith*, a 36-minute multimedia experience that tells the life story of Oral Roberts and 'encourages the potential of faith in your life'.

The campus of Oral Roberts University could have been transplanted from the pre-war Brussels Exhibition. Each building is a pavilion with a different theme and texture. ORU's Mabee Center, designed like two flattened kettle drums, is Oklahoma's largest indoor sports arena, with a seating capacity of 10,500. It is also used for opera, theatre and symphony concerts, and was built at a cost of five and a half million dollars. The John D. Messick

Learning Resources Center looks like a Saudi Arabian palace and contains more than 15 acres of floor space for the graduate and professional schools of the university. On the campus there is a University Village Retirement Center. The Oral Roberts Ministry offers a variety of financial services to the elderly, including a life income agreement and a gift annuity plan.

At ORU there are dormitory towers, acres of car parking, arenas covered by graceful low geodesic domes, and high classroom blocks built like the spokes of a wheel. Fundamental to the whole enterprise is the big Roberts television complex; but the inevitable satellite uplink dishes look quite insignificant amid so much shining grandeur. This is a city for Superman—garish but striking. From the air it has a Martian geometry of stars, cubes, diamonds and circles. All it lacks is a space shuttle or two which would enable Oral Roberts to launch his very own satellites.

The university was dedicated by Roberts's 'warm friend' Billy Graham in 1967 before 18,000 people. On Graduation Day 1985, President Roberts in his academic regalia watched with pride as 906 graduates walked across the platform to receive their degrees. 'My heart nearly burst from my body,' he wrote. They included 49 physicians, 30 dentists, 50 registered nurses, 64 young men and women from the graduate school of theology preparing to serve in more than 30 denominations and independent groups, 75 teachers, 46 lawyers and over 200 business school graduates. As well as receiving a diploma, each graduate was personally greeted by son and heir-apparent Richard Roberts, also looking suitably cerebral.

The surprising discovery at ORU is that the atmosphere is so normal. Classrooms are refreshingly untidy, the staff are highly qualified and far from fanatical, and among the students are Catholics and Episcopalians. Some ORU faculties enjoy a high reputation in the United States. The graduate school of theology is recognised by the United Methodist Church.

Feelings for President Roberts are ambivalent. There is admiration for his sincerity and vigour but a scepticism about his ability to listen. The viability of the City of Faith Healing Center is often questioned. Richard Roberts has had a difficult start, but if the Roberts empire is to outlive its emperor, there has to be a successor. Richard is presented to the world as an evangelist with healing insights. A battery of telephones ring behind him as he makes his televised prayer for the sick. It's almost a seance. There's a lady here and a man there with backache or a shoulder pain or something. Roberts Junior screws his eyes even tighter. He cannot quite visualise the problem of this or that anonymous viewer. 'Give it all to me, Father,' he cries. The picture clears in his mind and another – totally unverifiable—miracle takes places before some distant TV screen.

To be the son of an evangelist is an interesting concept. In this mortal world it will ensure a future for the healing center, ORU and the Roberts Evangelistic Association. The Tulsa staff view Richard Roberts with mixed feelings. There is sympathy for what must have been an unusual up-bringing, embarrassment over his divorce, and some relief that he has gained a television persona that may just be enough to keep the show on the road.

As well as health in body and spirit, the Oral Roberts organisation requires a healthy donor base—a huge group of people scattered across the nation who will watch the programmes and be moved to make donations and buy the books, tapes and magazines. Oral's supporters are growing old with him. The hope is that Richard will be able to relight the lamp for his generation. It would be a daunting task for anyone. In the summer of 1985 there was a 'financial emergency' at ORU. So whatever their innermost feelings, the fervent prayer of the Tulsa professionals has to be a suitably American version of 'God Bless the Prince of Wales'.

In her book *Ashes to Gold*, Patti Roberts tells the story of her failed marriage to Richard. She writes: 'I was frightened for Richard and for us. Oral always said that success without a successor was failure, and I began to feel that we were being re-created in his image. We were to be the second generation Oral and Evelyn. Richard wasn't Richard; he was Oral with another name—Oral at age twenty-five again. But, unfortunately, I wasn't Evelyn, and therein lay a large part of the problem.'

From *Ashes to Gold* by Patti Roberts with Sherry Andrews, copyright © 1983 by Patti Roberts; used with permission of Word Books, Publisher, Waco, Texas, USA.

Patti says she is not anti-Oral Roberts: 'There's a lot of God in Oral, a lot of creativity. He's a wonderful, wonderful person.' She describes the opulent lifestyle, the 'great personal excesses' allowed to her as a member of one of America's foremost Christian empires. She remembers her bathroom: the tub itself was seven feet long, with a gold swan for a tap and, directly over it, a gold and crystal chandelier. The room was decorated with mirrors and Chinese wallpaper. It had a thick yellow carpet, a chaise longue and three telephones.

She describes the paradox of American religious broadcasting: 'Television enabled us to reach more people, it also allowed us to remain very remote. Public meetings and concerts bring you into direct contact with hurting, needy people. Television insulates you from them. You tape the shows, and by the time they air, you are in Palm Springs vacationing.' She closes her bestseller with a plea: 'Don't forget or negate the truly wonderful accomplishments of Oral Roberts simply because he is human, with human weaknesses.'

It is said of William Booth, the founder of the Salvation Army, that on his deathbed he ordered his son Bramwell to keep the faith or 'I will come back and haunt you'. Oral Roberts, while still in good health, went one step further. According to Patti Roberts, she and her bridegroom were sent off on their honeymoon with the dire warning that if either of them ever left Oral's ministry or turned their backs on God, they would be killed in a plane crash. Oral Roberts had had a dream.

In some ways he resembles Booth. There is the same passion, the same indifference to ridicule and the same dogmatism. He has the look of a farmer. As a youth he was shy; but now his circle of friends includes politicians and industrialists from the power centres of the American establishment. He does not raise all his funds from his television audience. He has been able to attract considerable corporate donations and endowments.

Oral Roberts's personal theology is best summed up in his book *Miracles of Seed-Faith*. This doctrine came to him while he was driving in the North West of the United States. He says it has changed his life. He teaches that giving makes things happen. Whatever you can conceive, and believe, you can do. God had the faith to plant the greatest seed of all, Jesus Christ. This divine act makes redemption possible. The Christian response must be to return seeds to God and there will be good results—always.

Seed-faith is the recurring theme on the Roberts television and radio shows. The teaching goes much further than tithing or Christian stewardship. Giving to God is the primary activity of his children. If you give to God you can expect a miracle. It always works. Something good is going to happen to you. But you must give even out of your need.

A cynic would immediately notice that seed-faith is a wonderfully convenient major theme for a religious broadcaster who relies on the cash donations of his audience. A disciple, on the other hand, will point out that the tens of millions of dollars that have flowed towards Oral Roberts have not been salted away but are there for all to see in the amazing buildings and institutions of his Tulsa theocracy.

As well as majoring on seed-faith, Oral Roberts has developed a rather unlovely language to explain it. His expressions include 'attack our lack', 'faith-walk', 'faith talk', 'God's SHALL-SUPPLY PROMISE', 'blessing-pact partnership' and even 'pre-' and 'post-blessing-pact'. 'They got their learning but they kept their burning,' he says proudly of his students.

Roberts-speak is tiring to the untutored ear but the meaning is usually crystal clear. One of his ventures costs 48 dollars per square foot. 'I need your help,' he says. 'Will you do it? Would you plant a seed—out of your need—and expect a miracle back from God?'

He publishes a special edition of the Bible with a personal, 259-page commentary. It is *not* for sale. 'God impressed me to send it as a gift to everyone who makes a Seed-Faith commitment of $120 for the ongoing work at the City of Faith Medical and Research Center where medicine and prayer are combined for the healing of millions.'

Oral Roberts is no great saint; but then again he is no great rogue. He may well go down in history as one of the twentieth century's greatest salesmen. The great edifices in Tulsa are convincing enough monuments to his courage. But his ministry has been a mission impossible. He has spent much of his life and most of his energy on an objective that cannot be achieved. It is impossible to hug children or kiss someone by television. It is equally impossible, even by throwing money at the problem, to transpose into mass media a caring, pastoral and healing ministry. Roberts has squared the circle by mass-producing and therefore vulgarising the healing gifts he claims to possess. He takes short cuts and has inevitably lost his way. Now he is trapped by the inexorable laws of accounting. He cannot go back to the simple life of the crusade tent, nor can he go forward without the enormous Oklahoman albatross that is tied to his neck. In Oral Roberts's Tulsa, two plus two has to make five. It is therefore a campus of contradictions: a holy city, new Jerusalem—but built on a fault line.

Postscript: On November 1, 1985, Oral Roberts announced an historic gift. The ORU law school, valued at $10 million and with a library of 200,000 volumes, would go to a new home in another Christian university some 24 hours (by car) from Tulsa. The law school has the largest collection of microfilmed legal documents in the United States. Oral Roberts has described it as the only Spirit-filled law school in the world. It would, he said, be given unconditionally to CBN University in Virginia Beach.

Chapter 7

Twenty-four hours from Tulsa

Nowadays it's average-sized, just one among 50 others. But once, when there were only 13 states, the Commonwealth of Virginia was the largest and the most populous and in every way the grandest. To the puritans of New England, the Virginian plantation owners were slave-owning nabobs; but they threw in their lot with the revolution against the British and they gave to the United States her first, third and fourth Presidents. When North and South were torn apart in civil war, more than half the battles took place on Virginian soil.

On April 29, 1607, 13 years before the Mayflower, 105 Englishmen made a permanent settlement in Virginia. They disembarked on Cape Henry in what is now the resort city of Virginia Beach. Their chaplain was the Reverend Robert Hunt, 'an honest, religious and courageous Divine'. The settlers made a covenant that 'from these very shores the Gospel shall go forth to not only this new world, but the entire world'.

Our only picture of the landing is an artist's impression. A simple wooden cross overlooks the ocean. Captain John Smith and his men kneel on the beach while a rather windswept Robert Hunt, in Anglican surplice and cope, says prayers of thanksgiving. Today there is an extra wooden cross in Virginia Beach, and it stands outside the headquarters of CBN, the Christian Broadcasting Cable Network. Its founder, Pat Robertson, is one of Hunt's descendants.

CBN's buildings are far removed from Tulsa's

● *CBN headquarters, Virginia Beach*

City of Faith. In Virginia Beach, well-groomed executives in sober suits preside quietly over a multi-million-dollar business. They carry themselves like decorous and conservative bank executives. If the flashy Oral Roberts complex looks as if its architect was Cecil B. De Mille, the CBN buildings are pure colonial Williamsburg. On the outside, America's largest Christian broadcasting network is Virginian and the gentleman in charge comes from the Commonwealth's top-drawer.

Pat Robertson is a preacher, a politician and patrician. He is a tall, well-built man. His good looks have improved with middle age. He has a youthful, almost cherubic face. Smiling suits him; and he smiles most of the time. This handsome man who looks like a Kennedy comes from a political family. He is the son of a US senator who became chairman of the Senate Banking and Currency Committee. According to Pat Robertson, his father was not wealthy but was a Washington politician who had to make do on his salary.

Robertson Junior made an impressive start in life. He went to a military prep school; he saw combat in Korea as a Marine officer; he took a degree in law from Yale. By 1956, he was a partner in an electronics component business and involved in New

• *Pat Robertson: patrician*

York Democratic Party politics. He lived on Staten Island with his wife Dede. He had the looks, the background and the contacts to be a high flyer in business or politics.

But his life began to turn sour. He became dissatisfied with his sophisticated lifestyle. He failed the New York Bar examinations. Life seemed empty and futile. He even contemplated suicide. Then his life began to take a Christian direction. His deeply religious mother was pleased. Dede had very mixed feelings. He tried several different denominations and came under the influence of a Dutch evangelist Cornelius Vanderbreggen. The search became a headlong rush towards God. Dede was soon left behind.

Pat Robertson felt, now that he had a personal relationship with Jesus, he would try to make restitution for what had been wrong with his life in the past. He sat down one night to try to make a list of everyone he had wronged. He remembered that in the Marines he had hitched a lift, ostensibly on military business, in a transport plane from Virginia to California. He calculated that he had defrauded the US Government of $165, and sent a cheque for that amount to the Marine Corps.

He went to Canada for a summer camp organised by the Inter-Varsity Fellowship. Dede, a graduate of the Yale University School of Nursing, told him that only someone with schizoid tendencies would leave his pregnant wife and young child to go to talk to God in the woods. Within two days she wrote to him pleading for him to return. His Bible 'fell open' at 1 Corinthians 7:32, 'But he that is married careth for the things that are of the world, how he may please his wife'. He wrote a short note to Dede telling her he could not leave the camp, but that God would look after her.

He enrolled in a Bible seminary in New York. His circle of friends included people from different countries who had experienced charismatic renewal and for whom personal conversion to Christ was not enough until it had been filled out with the gifts of the spirit, including the gift of tongues. He came under the influence of an energetic young Reformed Church minister, Harald Bredesen.

Robertson had been baptised 'as a boy' in his home church but it had not been 'believer's baptism'. He was re-baptised by Bredesen, who taught him to pray for yet another experience, a 'baptism in the Holy Spirit'. Pat and Dede Robertson are now spiritually synchronised. In the middle of one New York night, they knelt on a hard floor and, for the first time together, spoke in the mysterious and all-possessing language of tongues.

Robertson had made a modest but successful radio debut in his home state in Lexington. With $70 to his name, he managed to pull together $37,000 to buy a defunct television station in Tidewater Virginia. In January 1960, the former Stork Club swinger applied for the Christian Broadcasting Network of Portsmouth to become a non-profit corporation to 'spread the truths of the Holy Bible by any means'.

Almost as soon as they arrived, the Robertsons' charismatic convictions brought them into conflict with local churches. They were refused membership in one Baptist Church. The local mainline denominations would give no support to the new station. The greatest problems were financial; but on October 1, 1961, they went on the air with a signal so weak it scarcely reached three miles across the river to Norfolk.

From this shaky start, CBN has grown into an international satellite communications and production corporation. It is taken by 5,300 cable systems with a total potential audience of more than 27 million households and operates 24 hours a day. The empire now includes worldwide syndication of programmes, a Middle East television station, and CBN University.

In the United States, CBN is the nation's third largest cable network and seeks to be the 'family entertainer'. Programme schedules draw on classic movies, comedy and serious drama. There is also a CBN news service. There have been a number of scoops, including Rock Hudson's last interview, as well as an exclusive with Laura Walker Snyder, daughter of the spy John Anthony Walker Jr. Two years earlier the troubled Laura, who later reported her father to the FBI, had been helped by one of CBN's telephone counsellors.

One of the maxims of secular broadcasting is that there is a time and place for everything; and this includes religion. There are times when religious programmes are acceptable and other times when they will cause audience figures to fall. CBN knows when not to be evangelical. During weekdays, there may be two specifically Bible programmes in the early morning. During the rest of the day, apart from three screenings of *The 700 Club*, the hours are filled with light entertainment that is 'family-fit'. Schedules have included *Skippy the Bush Kangaroo*, *Bachelor Father*, *The Patty Duke Show*, *I Married Joan*, *The Man from U.N.C.L.E.* and *The Best of Groucho*.

Even on Sundays the realities of audience-building are respected. The day may begin with three chieftains of the Electronic Church—an hour with Jimmy Swaggart, followed by another with James Kennedy, followed by yet another with Kenneth Copeland. But CBN's Sunday morning schedules would be no more religious than some local television chanels. By midday, the Christian Network is changing its mood. *Wagon Train*, *Alias Smith and Jones* and *Doris Day's Best Friends* carry the network to mid-evening, when inspirational and evangelical programmes return.

CBN publishes a rather grandiloquent justification for what is really a diet of re-runs and old movies. Moral and spiritual decay is marching across the screens of America. A new frontier in Christian broadcasting is being forged. CBN is the family network that is refusing 'to compromise traditional Judaeo-Christian values'.

The flagship of the CBN fleet of programmes is its own *700 Club*. It is also the personal vehicle of Pat Robertson and a major source of finance for his network. In the beginning, Robertson recruited 700 members, each one giving 10 dollars. Nowadays the

club has more than half a million members nationwide, and the minimum monthly subscription is 15
dollars. Twice a year CBN tops up its finances
through fund-raising telethons. Together, Robertson's various businesses and charities bring in about
$230 million each year.

The 700 Club goes out from Virginia Beach five
days in every seven. It has a *Good Morning America*
feel about it. The set is comfortable and unostenta-
tious. There's an oriental carpet, a leather buttoned
sofa and a reassuring library backdrop without too
many books. Behind the tier of seating for the studio audience are dozens of telephone desks screened
by glass. Volunteers, many with open Bibles, mur-
mur advice to some of the network's 16,000 daily
callers.

The club is not presented as a one-man band.
Robertson's regular co-host and straightman is Ben
Kinchow. A 6ft 6in former Black Muslim, he is involved in a number of CBN's charitable projects.
Minutes before the programme begins, a swarm of
neatly-suited clipboard-carrying females buzz into
action. 'Do any of today's audience have any questions for Pat or Ben?' 'Please write your question on
the blue slip and pass it to the end of your row.'
Three minutes to ten, and a production assistant
gives friendly hints about how to be a friendly audience and then leads in prayer for the programme.
Forty-five seconds to lift-off. An even friendlier,
and beautifully tailored, Pat Robertson appears.
The ear-to-ear smile gives him a winning, dimpled
baby face. Time is short. He says a few well-chosen
words to the audience. Holdings hands with another of his co-hosts, the comely Denuta Soder-
man, he bows his head briefly in intercession. Half a
dozen hurried strides and he is sitting before the
camera where he has sat for most of his adult life. In
1965 it was estimated that Pat Robertson's cuddly
countenance regularly entered 7,200,000 American
homes. A Nielsen survey rated him the most popular of the nation's top ten television evangelists.

The 700 Club opens unexceptionally. There are reports from Congress and from abroad. There are

general interest features on dangerous medicines, financial updates and 'insights into today's uncertain economy'. CBN's theatre correspondent presents his recorded interview with the first lady of the American stage, Helen Hayes. Rhonda Fleming tells how God guides her life. But during the first third of the programme, religion is soft-pedalled. Denuta feeds Pat Robertson with questions about American domestic politics, arms control and international affairs. Some of his answers are long-winded and reveal the recurring artistic and editorial fault of all America's religious owner-presenters. Real control is in the hands of the man in front of the camera. He can talk as long as he likes on any subject, and often does. Few producers will dare to switch off the star who also owns the network. Pat Robertson is by no means the worst offender. Sometimes Paul Crouch, presenter/proprietor of Trinity Broadcasting Network, seems more interested in the reaction of some off-camera studio minion than in his special guest of the moment. Communication with his staff is of necessity non-verbal and gives him a tortured look.

Each edition of *The 700 Club* opens with general interest subjects. The final third of most programmes has Pat Robertson at full throttle, ministering to the viewers and answering Bible queries for the studio audience. The first and last styles are very different, and there has to be a central linking section composed of what the CBN professionals describe as 'crossover material'. The show contains two cleverly executed gear shifts. Without them, the enormous increase in spiritual tempo would come as the rudest of shocks.

By the end of the show there is a different Robertson on the screen. The man of the world with his self-deprecating humour and pithy political analysis is left behind. Everything that went before in the programme is revealed as a great softening-up exercise. With his eyes screwed up fiercely, Robertson has become the prophet of God and healer, and presents the viewers and their problems to their Creator. The muffled telephones tinkle. News of ailments and personal crises have been pouring into Virginia Beach. His voice shaking, this media-mediator prays fervently before the holy of holies for his absent friends.

Under the sugar coating and the Ivy League manners, Pat Robertson's healing ministry has closely resembled that of Oral Roberts. He too is given insights about the hernias and haemorrhoids of anonymous sufferers. He too praises the Lord fervently for unusual but unsubstantiated miracles.

Meanwhile, back in the lavishly furnished colonial-style mansion that is CBN's headquarters, the organisation purrs. Quiet groups of visitors from all over America troop respectfully across the marble floors of this purpose-built palace. They admire the antiques in the foyer and the huge, specially-woven carpet. Upstairs are gathered some of the 12 apostles. They are life-sized, and made of scrap metal. They were not expensive and are the best sight in the whole building. The tour ends in front of *The Flight into Egypt*. It is nearly 40ft long and seems uncertain about whether it is a painting or the backdrop for an opera.

Elsewhere in the CBN Center, the many-sided work of a big corporation continues. As well as the central task of maintaining airtime on thousands of American cable systems, the network is also an international business. Its animated children's programme *Superbook* has found a worldwide market, including Japanese Television and the BBC. Across the United States there are 90 CBN 'Help and Counselling Centers' staffed by four and a half thousand volunteers and handling over three million calls each year.

The Network has the inevitable 'Christian financial planning' department to help viewers dispose of their earthly assets in a tax-efficient manner that will enable the donor to 'honor the Lord'. CBN had a heavy involvement in the multi-million-dollar marketing of *THE BOOK*—a new, user-friendly edition of the Living Bible. Youthful executives, wise beyond their years, speak of markets and Nielsen and Arbitron surveys. Behind another door sit 'two

PhDs' doing 'nothing but research'.

Dr David Clark is the vice-president for marketing. Well respected by religious broadcasters in the mainline denominations, he is thought of as a 'thinking man's electronic churchman'. He maintains that the network's programmes are meeting needs, and that support comes from across the Christian spectrum. No, he does not believe entertainment is inherently incongruous with proclaiming the Gospel.

In the middle of the day the staff make their way quietly and in their hundreds to a circular chapel in the heart of the building. They gather quietly on low Roman benches set in concentric circles in a thickly carpeted and gently sunken floor. A short sermon, some prayers and a few restrained but spontaneous 'Amens', then the men and women of the Christian network re-emerge from their godly amphitheatre and once more get down to business.

Pat Robertson's success in television has allowed him to branch out. With 800 students, his university is much smaller than Oral Roberts University in Tulsa. However, there are graduate courses in communication, education, business administration, biblical studies, public policy, journalism and counselling. There are plans for considerable expansion. CBNU already has a $12 million library.

In 1978, CBN sponsored Operation Blessing to help the world's poor. The network claims half a million people have now received food aid and technical assistance from an 'action-army' of helpers. Pat Robertson is a vocal supporter of President Reagan's policy towards Nicaragua. Operation Blessing has raised $2 million for anti-Sandinista refugees.

Robertson also fosters the Freedom Council. It was founded in 1981 to keep watch on courtroom decisions on the separation of church and state. When Florida senior citizens are forbidden to sing a hymn before their federally-funded lunch, and when the Ten Commandments are removed from a Kentucky clasroom wall by court order, Robertson believes America is losing its religious liberties.

In 1985, he moved to the centre stage of national politics. Could the Commonwealth of Virginia, already the provider of eight Presidents, provide a ninth? Robertson the politician has moved a long way from the party of his senator father and from the days when he himself was chairman of the Stevenson-for-President headquarters on Staten Island. He is now a Reagan Republican wanting less government and strong defences against Communism.

For the Republicans, ROBERTSON IN '88 would be a mixed and far from divine blessing. There is no guarantee that other highly politicised television evangelists would fall in line behind a flag bearer from Virginia Beach. The secular networks would have a ball with resurrected video tapes of Robertson's lively healing sessions. His biblical exegesis makes him a political sitting duck.

Myra MacPherson of the *Washington Post* describes one 1981 show. 'Using a map and pointer, Robertson points to the Middle East. "I believe that the Bible indicates that ultimately Israel will take territory all the way up to the Euphrates River, which is north of Damascus. This might well be the trigger that would bring the Soviet Union down on Israel for an invasion that was spoken of in the book Ezekiel, Chapter 38." When Ben Kinchow goes on to suggest that the Tarshish who might come to the aid of Israel could be Americans, Robertson agrees that the "only time where the United States is talked about in the Bible is in connection with this area".'

He believes that only the will of God would send him to the White House, and that his job in Virginia Beach is better than any in Washington. Certainly he has made an enormous mark in American broadcasting. He was one of the very first in the Electronic Church to understand the importance of satellites. He is also indirectly responsible for a smaller, rival Christian network. PTL has its own superbly equipped studios in North Carolina, in its own reproduction-Williamsburg building and with its own PTL Club. Host and founder Jim Bakker was one of the original team at CBN. He freely admits his debt to Robertson.

Pat (his real Christian name is Marion) Robertson shields his personal life from publicity. Television rivals suggest he has made a fortune from his work; and one of them purported to show an aerial view of a well appointed estate. Pat Boone, singer and friend, supposes Robertson does not have very much money.

He is an elegant enigma: a right-wing idealogue who looks like a President; a velvet-smooth telegenic operator who could easily be cast as a soap opera clansman. But Pat Robertson is also a wide-eyed, open-mouthed charismatic. In his autobiography, this missionary in mohair speaks glowingly of a land of wonders. He tells of an anointing that has touched many areas of his life, and not least his broadcasting. On one occasion the Holy Spirit was so intensely present in the studio that a cameraman wept so much that there was a puddle of water on the floor. The programme stayed on the air until the early hours of the morning as the telephone operators received reports of miracles from far and wide.

Chapter 8

Roman holiday

'The People of God walk in history. As they, who are, essentially, both communicators and recipients, advance with their times, they look forward with confidence and even enthusiasm to whatever the development of communications in a space-age may have to offer.'—From the pastoral instruction for the application of the Decree on Social Communication of the Second Vatican Council.

The benign Presidency of Dwight D. Eisenhower was something of a turning point for the Catholic population of the United States. The white Anglo-Saxon Protestant ascendancy was crumbling. There was still plenty of scope for religious prejudice—and indeed for racialism as well—but Catholicism could no longer be perceived as an immigrant, somehow un-American, faith. Catholics were not after all strangers in their own land.

As a group they had been kept in their place not only by the actions and attitudes of the Protestant majority, but also by wave after wave of immigration which dissipated the Church's energies. It was only after the tide of immigration had dried up and the Catholic population had stabilised that the Church could step out of its role of protector and nursemaid to the most powerless group in American society.

In the inter-war years, the faithful, particularly the urban faithful, had three defenders—the Church, the Democratic Party and the labour unions. Catholic involvement in city politics had been essentially an exercise in mutual self defence against the twin enemies of bigotry and economic catastrophe. During these years, union membership was two-thirds Catholic.

There were already signs that Catholicism would one day emerge as the 'third great faith' of the United States. At the turn of the century there had been an 'Americanist' movement among some of the hierarchy; and 1928 almost marked a coming-of-age when, in a bitterly-fought presidential campaign, Al Smith, Governor of New York and a Catholic, took a creditable 40 per cent of the popular vote. Despite these stirrings and the supremacy of the Democratic Party from 1932, the Catholic Church of the United States continued to stand apart. This state of isolation could not be justified by the arithmetic. If all the non-Roman churches combined, they would outnumber Catholics, but by a factor of less than two to one. Catholicism is also the continent's most ancient Christian tradition, predating by many years the Virginia landings and the Mayflower Fathers.

Nevertheless Catholics felt separated from the rest of American life. Too often they had enjoyed meagre rewards from American capitalism. In order to survive they had evolved a separate system of education and health care. They had their own social and charitable institutions. In many cases they were America's most recent immigrants and lived out their lives without the English language. Despite their 'catholicism', they had to come to terms with each other—Irish with German, Ruthenian with Italian. The parish was a pot pourri of European cultures. American culture was supposedly somewhere else — and Protestant. A 'minority complex' prevented the Church from playing a full part in national life and in national broadcasting. A Protestant broadcaster could be 'evangelistic' while a Roman Catholic (outside the densely Catholic areas) would be a 'proselytiser'. Inevitably the first Catholic broadcaster to have a national reputation was best known for his politics rather than for his religion.

Charles E. Coughlin was born in Canada. He was ordained in 1916, and in the 1920s was working in the Detroit area. He was well known as a preacher and parish organiser. His devotion to the recently canonised St Theresa of the Little Flower gave him a local reputation on radio. In 1929 the Crash gave him a new theme. He became an ardent Roosevelt supporter; but his ardour soon cooled and he developed a series of economic remedies centring on the notion, shared by many Catholics worldwide, of the 'corporate state'. By 1936 he had 10 million weekly listeners and employed 124 clerks to handle mail and donations. After his break with FDR, the 'radio priest' became associated with anti-semitism. Eventually he ceased to be regarded as a serious Catholic broadcaster.

The genuine Catholic pioneer on American radio and television was Monsignor (later Archbishop) Fulton Sheen. In the 1940s he was the star of NBC's *Catholic Hour*. With charm and humour he presented a clear, straightforward gospel. Among his many converts were Henry Ford II, Claire Booth Luce and Louis Budenz, the Communist leader. In 1951, still with NBC, he repeated his success on television. On *Life is Worth Living* he had no props apart from a blackboard, a Bible and his eminently theatrical Roman robes.

A natural broadcaster, he had the gift of speaking directly to the individual viewer. His compelling eyes under prominent dark eyebrows gave him an enormous television presence and an appeal that crossed confessional boundaries. Fulton Sheen, scholar-broadcaster and for 17 years national director of the Society for the Propagation of the Faith, gave Catholicism its highest profile on America's growing number of television screens. He could attract as many as 6,000 letters a day. Each half-hour programme was meticulously prepared and rehearsed, and ended with the benediction 'God love you'.

Dr Ben Armstrong recalls introducing Archbishop Sheen as a guest at the 35th anniversary dinner of National Religious Broadcasters. The applause from 1,500 evangelical communicators was thunderous. Fulton Sheen had been a bright

• *Catholic star:*
Fulton Sheen

star in an otherwise Protestant firmament. He had presented a viable non-evangelical alternative that nowadays is no longer available to the viewer.

Fulton Sheen was in no way the first pope of a Catholic, viewer-sustained electronic church. His airtime was supported by an advertiser (Admiral). Indeed, he was paid a small fortune in fees, which he made over to his society. His was a unique appeal to a large audience. His personal following was non-transferable. He could have no imitators and no successor. He was not thrust forward by any ecclesiastical process. He was a star.

Looking back at the fifties and sixties, it is surprising to find that the decline in Protestant power did not lead to a period of Catholic self-assertion or even self-confidence. The effect — or rather, the lack of effect — on American broadcasting has been all-important. Roman Catholicism has lost its immigrant, alien image. For a quarter of a century it has stood in the American pantheon alongside Protestantism and Judaism. But paradoxically, the last 25 years have been years of soul searching, uncertainty and crisis.

For too many decades the Church had too high a fence around her flock. The motive, of course, was to protect and to differentiate; but within the well-defended boundary there had been little intellectual freedom and not enough outside influence. But for more than two decades the new all-American Catholics have been travelling out beyond their fence and, like released POWs, have been able to look back from a distance at their old home. They can now afford the time and space for reform and even revolution. They are in a New World at last; but unfortunately it is a world of their own.

Catholics are putting their old home in order; or, to put it less kindly, they are preoccupied with their own internal problems. They are no longer an embattled working class. The often nominally Catholic immigrant no longer needs an ecclesiastical protector. As many as 1,300,000 Hispanic Americans have discovered that they were never really Catholic at all. The pressure is off and the cracks are showing. These have been made even wider by an earthquake which has changed Catholicism on every continent. The epicentre was in Rome under an old and godly Pope who wanted to turn his church upside down. Vatican II had an immense—some would say devastating—effect on the American Church, in which by 1970 a radical spirit could be observed. The establishment was under siege and Rome's assailants were not latter-day Visigoths but Roman Catholics themselves. They had been conditioned far too long by what one journalist, John O'Connor, described as a 'velvet-gloved Renaissance terror'. They were determined on a radical renewal of their church.

Renewal continues. The American Catholic Church—the third largest in the world—goes its own way. Evangelism is left to the evangelicals and ecumenism to the mainline Protestants. Catholics are tolerant of the Electronic Church—much more tolerant than the mainliners—perhaps because they themselves cannot mobilise the energy or resources to participate on a scale that would be appropriate to their enormous numerical strength. Many North American Catholics would consider the Electronic Church to be a great deal better than nothing. Russell Shaw, influential spokesman for the National Conference of Catholic Bishops, makes a personal confession: 'When my wife and I want to quieten the kids, we routinely search out CBN for the simple reason that it is good bedrock Judaeo-Christian material.'

One of the fondest notions of liberal Protestants is that they occupy some kind of middle ground between Catholics and Conservative evangelicals. Their fantasy is of a religious spectrum with the Pope at one end and Jerry Falwell at the other, and with themselves bridging the gap and making dialogue possible. Nothing could be further from reality. There are no 'bridge churches'. If there has to be a diagram to express interdenominational links, it ought to be a triangle. Some Catholics have a great deal more in common with evangelicals than with liberals. The Electronic Church meets a widespread yearning for the once-Catholic virtues of clarity, certainty and enthusiasm. It satisfies those who still insist that religion ought to provide answers to questions.

The unwritten Catholic-evangelical alliance is a strictly North American phenomenon, and the result of a certain disenchantment with a new, liberalised Church. The situation in South and especially Central America is completely different. In the 1960s, the Vatican Council, and particularly the Medellin Conference, led the Church to a volte face. Once the ally of repressive dictatorships, clergy associated themselves with the oppressed. Liberation theology was born. The various 'national security' regimes, seeking wolves in sheep's clothing, identified Marxists in cassocks. Priests and nuns began to die for their faith. The Rockefeller report on Latin America of 1969–1970 stated that the Catholic Church had ceased to be an ally in whom the United States could have confidence.

An edition of the Catholic bulletin *Pro Mundi Vita*, published in Brussels in 1985, suggested that one result of the Rockefeller report was a recommendation to the United States Government for an extensive campaign with the aim of propagating Protestant churches and conservative sects in Latin America. The Bulletin identified the 1970s as the period which had seen the greatest expansion of sectarian Protestantism in the history of South America. One of *Pro Mundi Vita's* judgments was particularly memorable: it expressed a deep resentment at the undoubted impact of the North American Electronic Church. The bulletin spoke of a 'sectarian environment' in which it found the 'religious transnationals' (World Vision International, Campus Crusade for Christ, PTL, the Billy Graham Evangelistic Association, the 700 Club and others). Their aim was seen as ideological and political rather than religious. They had few leaders, and those they did have were notable for their militancy.

But North of the Rio Grande there is lack of enmity and an altogether unlikely harmony between Catholics and evangelicals. Dr David Clarke, vice-president of marketing for CBN, estimates that 30 per cent of his network's viewers and 20 per cent of its donors are Catholics. These figures are borne out and even improved upon by Catholic broadcasters. Karl Holtsnider, executive vice-president of the Franciscan Communications Center in Los Angeles, believes up to 35 per cent of contributors to some television evangelists also attend Mass each week.

Not wishing to bite the hand that feeds them, most televangelists avoid anti-Catholic comments. They also avoid pro-Catholic comments. There is simply silence. Several Catholic broadcasting agencies have links with National Religious Broadcasters and are listed in the NRB directory. Always the maverick, the engaging Robert Schuller positively rejoices in his link with Rome. A picture of the ever-positive Dr Robert meeting the Pope adorns the visitors' centre at the Crystal Cathedral. The North American Catholic hierarchy displays an almost trancelike equanimity about the Electronic Church—even towards those evangelicals who are making considerable gains among the Hispanic population of the United States (already the world's fourth largest). Many of the leaders of the Electronic Church are heavily involved in this mission to proselytise among so many nominal Catholics. They hope that by the end of the decade there will be two million Hispanic Protestants in the country. The only counter-measures have come from bishops (mainly in the South West) whose dioceses are in the front line.

It is one of the ironies of ecclesiastical life that a seemingly centralised organisation such as the American Catholic Church can exhibit such distinctly congregationalist tendencies. On the other hand, an institution steeped in the traditions of local independence, the Southern Baptist Convention can, and does, behave as a well co-ordinated national denomination. Put bluntly, it is very difficult to fund any national Catholic project, including broadcasting.

The Church's commitment to satellite communications is partial and hesitant. Only 70 of the 170 American dioceses participate on a regular basis in the Catholic Telecommunications Network of America (CTNA). Financing of this for-profit corporation was sufficient for the cost of the hardware, but few resources remain for programming. Nevertheless, the decision to proceed was courageous. Episcopal control was preserved. To prevent radical theologians arriving uninvited on the screens of his diocese, each downlink is under the direct control of the local bishop.

The ancient system of largely autonomous dioceses prevents the Church from behaving as a coordinated unit. The evidence of Roman and non-Roman churches alike suggests that there will never be the budgets or the trained personnel to enter the world of big-time broadcasting. An Episcopalian broadcaster sums up the problem of the men and women in the various national headquarters: 'Too often they are forced into serving as promotional arms for the denomination and publicity channels for current programmes and issues.' There are many in the American Catholic Church who are aware of the problem. It has long been obvious that the most successful Catholic media projects are those undertaken by what one report calls the 'independent syndicators'—Paulists, Marianists, Franciscans, Redemptorists, Christophers and, here and there, highly motivated diocesan communications teams.

America's religious communities are in some ways unique in the Catholic Church. Most of them are rooted in the sometimes frantic drive to provide an educational service for huge immigrant congregations. There are about 1,000 religious communities in the United States with 150,000 members, four fifths of them female. The Paulists are home-grown, founded by an American to preach to Americans. They are autonomous and therefore quickly adaptable to new situations. It is no accident that Paulist Productions are the liveliest communicators in the Church and have the best links with Hollywood's directors and actors. In many local situations, Catholic communicators are ideal-

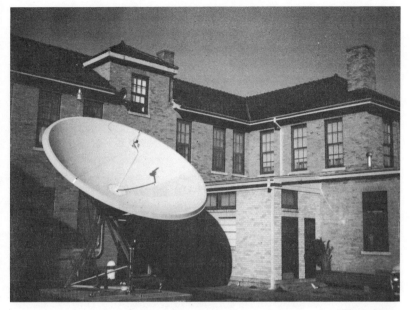

● *The Archbishop
Fulton Sheen Center:
a wide reputation*

istic and energetic. ITP (Intercommunity Telecommunications Project) is a Maryland-based coalition
of Paulist and Redemptorist broadcasters committed to trying to harness the latest technology to
the service of the Church. It is planning the production of a half-million-dollar coast-to-coast satellite
teleconference.

The Diocese of Tucson has its own television
station. Loyola University in New Orleans also has
its own station, and it is affiliated to CBS. The
Archbishop Fulton Sheen Center was founded by
Catholic charismatics and serves the dioceses of
Dallas and Fort Worth. Its reputation extends
across denominational barriers. It is the contractor
to the Billy Graham Evangelistic Association for
post-production television work. The centre's long-
time director, Deacon Steve Landregan, has his
own explanation for his organisation's highly professional output. 'Catholics have a different attitude
in the South West,' he says. 'We are a small minority church here and have to work for our living.' In
1985, a much-acclaimed Paulist programme, *The
Other Wise Man*, sponsored by Procter and Gamble,

was bought by ABC. The Diocese of Corpus Christi has two FM radio stations; and Brownsville Diocese operates a PBS station. There are training centres for Third World broadcasters; Spanish language programmes; and schools of communication attached to universities and seminaries. The Mass is televised daily in Boston, paid for by the viewers.

These are just some of a number—a large number—of telecommunications projects sponsored by the Church across America. But the result on the nation's television screens scarcely represents a church with more than 50 million members; a church that is four times larger than its runner-up. In the words of one combative priest, 'We ought to be able to knock those guys right off the screen.' The evangelical television preachers will continue to dominate prime-time broadcasting. Despite their smaller constituency, they alone can secure the immense funds that are needed to buy time on American television.

The problem is almost entirely one of dollars; but there has been among non-evangelicals an additional problem of amateurism. According to the Rev Louis Schueddig, most electronic media programmes in the Episcopal Church are produced by hobbyists, well-intentioned laity who enjoy working with cameras and editing equipment. Father John Geaney, former president of Unda-USA, the American branch of the international association for Catholic broadcasters, agrees. 'Too frequently local producers are not well trained for the tasks they are asked to fulfil for the Church. Allowing well-intentioned people, rather than well-intentioned skilful people, to create programming for the Church is to render a disservice to the Gospel.'

Several Catholic broadcasting ventures have failed spectacularly. Santa Fe Communications was planned as a satellite-delivered cable television service. It took a Catholic charismatic approach to programming and aimed at family orientated programmes such as *Bless Me Father*, *The Sullivans* and *Heart of the Nation*. Lack of cable system acceptance of the programming, and financial problems,

resulted in closure in 1985. Channel 46 in Los
Angeles is owned by the DeRancé Foundation. It is
claimed that $100 million has been pumped into
this station, which presents an antique, pre-Vatican
Council Catholicism. Court orders, disputes and
dwindling finances have made its future uncertain.
No American Catholic has yet reoccupied the position vacated by Fulton Sheen. The new economics
of broadcasting mean that charisma and even talent
are not enough. Coast-to-coast exposure is now only
possible to those who can pay to be seen. But there
are some Catholics who are trying to break into the
system.

• *John Bertolucci:
exuberant*

Father John Bertolucci is a big man with an
exuberant style. He is an unlikely amalgam of Franciscan professor and old-time revivalist. Many who
see him in action are struck by his highly evangelical vocabulary and his very Roman Catholic ap-
pearance. He believes 'personal evangelism is the
greatest need in the world today'. He is a charismatic who believes a 'full gospel'. Holding aloft a large
Bible, he can exhort his audience to 'believe the
Word'. One well placed observer considers Bertolucci to be among the Church's five greatest contemporary preachers. He was the only priest from
the United States to be invited to speak at the international youth conference held in Rome in 1984 and
attended by 50,000 people. His *Glory to God* television series is carried on both the PTL and TBN
cable networks. He has been described as the
Catholic Billy Graham. His St Francis Association
for Catholic Evangelism (FACE) also sponsors a
nationally syndicated radio programme called *Let
Me Sow Love*. FACE has a well-equipped radio studio on the campus of the Franciscan University of
Steubenville, Ohio. Bertolucci's television ministry
is based on the Archbishop Fulton Sheen Center in
Dallas.

The biggest name of all in Catholic broadcasting
is also Franciscan. Mother Angelica is the only
member of her communion to have approached
anywhere near the front rank of the Electronic
Church. She breaks every rule in the television

handbook. She is the wrong side of sixty. Her technique on camera is so straightforward as to be abrupt. An old spinal problem forces her to wear a leg brace, which she makes no effort to disguise from the viewer. She has the mildly intimidating manner of a maiden aunt who won't stand any nonsense. Her brown habit and the oversized crucifix hanging from her neck are not there to enhance her television persona. These are her working clothes, not studio props in the style of the elegant Archbishop Sheen. Mother Angelica is startlingly homespun. She treats her television audience with a matter-of-fact friendliness and humour; but she seems to make no extra special effort to be hospitable. She is down to earth and seemingly quite unpractised in feminine guile. Hers is a 'take me as you find me' performance.

Angelica is totally different from any other televangelist. She is different because she is so ordinary. Her achievements, however, have been far from ordinary. She is the founder and superior of Our Lady of the Angels Monastery near Birmingham, Alabama. There are a dozen nuns, one of whom is her own mother. A large printing plant turns out 20,000 items each day. The monastery, on the eastern reaches of Shades Crest Mountain, is also the national headquarters for Mother Angelica's Eternal Word Television Network.

She made a start in broadcasting with programmes for CBN. She was videotaping her show at a local commercial station when she became involved in a fierce argument with its manager for scheduling the movie *The Word*, which she considered to be blasphemous. She recalls the event: 'I told him I wouldn't do any more broadcasts at his station, that I'd build my own station.'

In 1981, Silvio Cardinal Oddi, Prefect of the Congregation for the Clergy, journeyed from Rome to Alabama to bless, as he put it, 'the satellite dish through which the Eternal Word is projected from ocean to ocean'. Cameras at the monastery are of the latest design. Broadcast equipment is sophisticated and state of the art. EWTN began by using the

Westar III Satellite but has now acquired a new position on Satcom IIIR, Transponder 18. The 'network' is available for four hours each evening, seven days a week. EWTN carried the programmes of Ralph Martin, Father Michael Manning, and Father Bertolucci. The 'network' itself produces a series entitled *Catholic Beliefs and Practices*. Repeats of old programmes include *The Bill Cosby Show* and Fulton Sheen's *Life Is Worth Living*.

Hers is an immense personal achievement. Mother Angelica buys her equipment on optimism and little else. Her faith and energy have brought her very favourable coverage on real network television. She hates asking for money from the viewers. Fund-raising telethons have been held to meet a series of five $100,000 payments for satellite time. Apart from anno domini, money would seem to be the only thing standing between her and a 24-hour television service. Why then is not the American Catholic Church throwing money in her direction?

The answer again is that despite its huge numerical strength the Church finds it well-nigh impossible to act as a co-ordinated national organisation. Mother Angelica (born Rita Francis) speaks of her own baptism in the Holy Spirit, but she is more identified with a conservative Catholicism that is out of favour with many bishops. She aims to translate Catholic spirituality into television terms, including the rosary and the Pope's weekly recitation of the Angelus. Readers of some of her literature are told that it is 'piously believed that those who recite this prayer 15 times daily ... will receive what they ask'. She is light years removed from her liberated and vocal sisters in orders who are almost at war with the Vatican over the Church's attitude to social and moral issues—even abortion. But she has her episcopal supporters—many of them—and a growing army of fans. She knows the cable television business and is well-versed in 'strongarming' techniques. She advises her audience to call the cable companies and DEMAND EWTN. 'Put the screw on 'em,' she says. 'Call 'em three times a week.'

Chapter 9

Mainline connection

He died a Church of England priest but he is counted as the founder of Methodism. If he had lived out his long life in the twentieth century rather than the eighteenth, he would undoubtedly be a master of satellite-to-cable television. As an evangelist in Georgia, he preached against sin, gin and the slave trade. Thirty-one years later, a Methodist chapel was opened in New York; and it was his ordination of a superintendent or bishop for this congregation that marked the beginning of the end of Methodism as a movement within the Church of England. Was he a Methodist or was he an Anglican? Perhaps he was both. If so, the twin churches of the evangelical Mr Wesley are nowadays firmly within the mainline fold. As such, in the vital area of broadcasting they continue to be eclipsed by the Electronic Church.

With two and a half million members, the American branch of Anglicanism is only one quarter the size of the United Methodist Church. But Episcopalians have had a much greater influence than their numbers alone would suggest. They are particularly well represented in the upper reaches of American society and among the decision makers in politics, diplomacy, business and banking. In recent years there has been a decline in numbers. The ordination of women priests has caused a split. Conservatives have been alienated in equal measure by prayer book revision and clergy radicalism. Most Episcopal parishes are not remarkably wealthy. Some have to struggle. But scattered across America are a dozen or so heavily endowed parishes with the

financial resources to make an impact in regional
broadcasting.

In a financial class of its own, and with a budget
exceeding that of the Episcopal Church itself, is
Trinity Church on New York's Wall Street. Often
called the richest church in the world, Trinity is a
Christian Croesus. It owes it all to Queen Anne,
who came to the throne of England in the year before John Wesley was born. She presented Trinity
Parish with a farm in what is now Lower Manhattan. The church still owns four per cent of the
original acreage, near the Holland Tunnel. It is
an astronomically wealthy institution, with a staff of
15 priests and with 350 lay employees involved
in estate management. The parish has problems as
well as great advantages. To avoid the charge of
being a real estate company that holds Sunday services, it retains (of all things!) a regular, inter-racial
congregation of several hundred. This itself is no
mean achievement. An incongruous Gothic doll's
house, it is sandwiched between the ziggurats of
New York capitalism. On Sunday the area is quiet.
On Ash Wednesday, 13,000 office workers and ty-
coons set foot on this ecclesiastical island without
the sun.

Trinity parish disposes of its wealth through a
grants board. Appropriate to its position on Wall
Street, there is a Trinity Center for Ethics and
Corporate Policy. There are Third World projects,
a school, a book store, a Christian education programme with 100 courses, and a Trinity Institute
which each year provides a continuing education
service to one out of ten of the country's Episcopal
clergy. According to one priest on the staff, there is
an 'incredible' sense of stewardship. 'Each year, we
more or less spend what we make.' The office of
communication oversees everything from business
cards to parish magazines. Its director, the Rev
Leonard Freeman, also believes his department
could be a 'a kind of research and development arm
for the Anglican Church—a place to try things out'.
The church's suite of offices near the New York
Stock Exchange now include a single but superbly

equipped television recording studio. 'You don't need many facilities like this,' claims Freeman. 'And in fact, it's the only one of its type that I know of in the Episcopal Church. But that's all right, as long as we can work co-operatively with each other.' His main television outlet has been through a New York City public service channel. The *Searching* series which he hosts covers a great variety of topics, including clergy burnout, averting nuclear war, ministry to prostitutes, 'Cotton Patch Gospel', prayer in the public schools, and Desmond Tutu.

One of Freeman's convictions about religious television is that the people who watch are religious already, or are open to the possibility of becoming so. This means that mainline religious broadcasters are wrong if they try too hard to be 'relevant'. 'If we are doing religious TV, we should say something religious, and the last place to say it is on Sunday morning.' Freeman is realistic about the economics of his television work and does not expect that Trinity Church's broadcasting will make a profit— ever. What he does foresee is that 'the differential will become reasonable' and that 'when you look at the difference you will be able to say—that's a reasonable cost for doing one heck of a lot of mission and ministry'.

475 Riverside Drive, New York City's ecumenical office block beside the Hudson, was dedicated by an Episcopal bishop. However, his church did not join in leasing office space in the new building. Instead the Episcopalians have their own church centre. It is on the East Side of Manhattan, on Second Avenue, and very close to the United Nations. The Office of Communications produces 10-, 30- and 60-second spots which can be used to promote the Episcopal cause on public service broadcasting. Alternatively, a parish or diocese can buy its own airtime and 'put on its own tag line'.

The Church co-operates with three other denominations, United Lutherans, Presbyterians and Disciples of Christ, to produce *One In The Spirit*. Despite its ecumenical title, this is not a joint production with a common editorial policy, but a se-

quence of programmes, each church waiting its turn.
According to Canon Richard Anderson, executive
for communication, the aim is 'basically feeding the
faithful but to do it in such a way that if a stranger
wanders in, he's not turned off by language, style
and a sense of clubbiness'. Programmes are made
on location and are not simply talking heads. *One In
The Spirit* reaches 250 cable systems via the Satcom
III satellite. Episcopal editions have included
'Families Matter', 'The TV Generation Discovers
Church Video' and, appropriately for a church so
pre-occupied with sexual equality, 'A Woman's
Place'.

Like similar agencies in most of the mainline denominations, the Episcopal Office of Communications lacks the resources or desire to compete with
the Electronic Church. The office has a staff of 18,
and its raison d'etre is to be a press office and to
oversee the production of a multitude of publications as well as representing the Church to the
major broadcasting networks. Its strategy is based
on the belief that 'communication of the Gospel
takes place primarily and most importantly in and
through local congregations of Christian people'.

Even if they wished to, could Episcopalians ever
compete with the Electronic Church? Richard
Anderson thinks not. The annual cost on network
television of a weekly one-hour programme from
Washington Cathedral would be $12 million. That
is more than half the national budget of the Episcopal Church. Even if the money could be found,
Anderson doubts whether 'impressed' viewers
would then 'go down to St George's Episcopal
Church'. 'It would, of course, make Episcopalians
feel good—but at what a cost!' He himself is
unimpressed with the underlying message of the
TV preachers, who he sees as 'success-orientated'.
'Over and over again we hear it: "I was in the gutter
and my life was a mess, and God has rewarded me
for having made this change." But you know it's
not true every time. The Church exists to be with
people whose life is hell for ever—those whose religious experience is genuine but who stay bankrupt.'

A third element in Episcopal broadcasting is neither a parish nor a central agency of the Church but the independent and self-supporting Episcopal Radio-TV Foundation. With an annual budget of about $600,000 and a staff of ten, the foundation is involved in various media projects and publishes a catalogue of audio-visual resources for the Church. It holds the North American film and video rights for the books of C.S. Lewis. With the United Methodist Church, the Presbyterian Church in the US and the Lutheran Church of America, it has produced *Perspectives*, an award-winning series of half-hour programmes for television. With Trinity Church, New York, and the National Office of Communications, the foundation is forming an Episcopal Television Group for the joint marketing of programmes.

For several reasons, Atlanta is an important centre for American telecommunications. Eighty per cent of the country's satellite broadcast equipment is produced in the city. It is also the headquarters of CNN, Ted Turner's 24-hour all-news network. As well as being the base for the Episcopal Radio-TV Foundation, it is also home to the Protestant Radio and Television Center. A considerable figure in the Electronic Church, Dr Charles F. Stanley, is pastor of First Baptist Church in the City. Born from the ashes of the Civil War, St Luke's, Atlanta, is a thriving downtown parish with a broadcasting tradition that goes back to the 1930s. Each Sunday, the mid-morning Eucharist is televised. It is transmitted from a microwave dish on the side of the church to the tower of one of the city's independent UHF stations. In a labyrinth of rooms and corridors beneath the church is a control centre, modest by the state-of-the-art standards of the Electronic Church. The parish is also involved in the city's cable television through Atlanta Interfaith Broadcasters, an ecumenical coalition. By Episcopal standards, St Luke's is something of a megachurch, and was once a cathedral. It has a staff of eight full-time priests, and a Sunday congregation of more than 2,000, with a further 4,000 to 5,000 watching the televised service. Already strongly committed to television in his previous parish, in Tennessee, the Rector, Dan Matthews, has a dream of a national television network that will communicate the Gospel 'according to the Anglican ethos'. The plan is to link 100 major Episcopal churches in the ownership of what may well be called the National Parish Network (NPN) and to purchase or lease a transponder on a satellite which would cover the entire country with its signal.

Fifteen churches have already indicated enthusiasm for the network. Among them are parishes that have been particularly well endowed by both God and mammon, including St Paul's Indianapolis (pharmaceuticals), Christchurch, Cincinatti (detergents), and St John the Divine, Houston (oil). At a meeting at Chicago's O'Hare Airport in July 1985, the project's clerical supporters agreed unanimously that 'the time is right for the Episcopal Church to move into television'. Time will tell. They have a highly professional full-time researcher. The financial commitment of St Luke's, Atlanta, already exceeds $60,000. Their plan is for an organisation that, although Episcopal, will be separate and autonomous. Their optimism contrasts with the interim report of the Presiding Bishop's Task Force on Satellite Communication, prepared in Berkeley, California, which has proposed further study and surveys.

Dan Matthews is an unusually zealous moderate. He believes that, with the plethora of television evangelists, it is no wonder they have captured so much attention. He believes it is time for the mainline alternative to be presented to the tens of millions of people who do not find the born-again idea to be plausible. He can now be more influential in the Episcopal Church, as Rector of Trinity Church, New York City.

The Episcopalians' first — and nowadays far more numerous—cousins are mostly gathered in the United Methodist Church. It was formed in 1968 by a merger with the Evangelical United Brethren. The roots of both partners in the union are intertwined in the eighteenth century; and from their beginnings, both emphasised personal and social holiness. The reason why they existed for so long as separate if parallel churches was neither doctrinal nor structural, but ethnic. The history of one group began among English-speaking Americans, and that of the other among the neglected German-speaking settlers in the Middle Colonies.

Today, the United Methodist Church is one of the two largest Protestant denominations in the United States, with 9,300,000 members in 38,000 congregations. It is second only to the mighty Southern Baptist Convention. But this united church still does not include every American group that looks back to John Wesley as its founder. Large denominations outside the union include Wesleyan and Black Methodists and the Church of the Nazarene. Nevertheless, the United Methodist Church has a nationwide organisational coverage. The denomination is the most racially diverse of all the mainline churches and has within its membership a considerable number of black, Hispanic, Asian and native Americans.

Of all Christians, Methodists are the least afflicted by the 'True Church Syndrome'. But there are no specifically *Methodist* doctrines to exercise a centripetal force upon the denomination. To compensate, they have established their identity through an emphasis on organisation and system that is second to none. United Methodist Communications (UMCom) is one of the Church's 14 national agencies. Its headquarters and production studios are located in Nashville. This is also the base for Ecufilm, which, as its name suggests, serves several different denominations. From its offices in Evanston, the church's communicators concentrate on the task of informing supporters and church members how their dollars are being spent. This activity goes under the altogether unlovely title of 'Program and Benevolence Interpretation'. The Church's broadcasting work is centred on Nashville and also (where else?) the 13th floor of John D. Rockefeller's magnificent gift to American ecumenism, 475 Riverside Drive, New York City.

Sharing the same floor is MARC, the Media
Action Research Center, Inc. It was established
in 1974 with a grant from the United Methodist
Church to study the impact of television on viewers,
and to work for positive changes in the broadcasting system. Both MARC and its parent, United
Methodist Communications, emphasise media
education. There is little ambition to mimic the
Electronic Church; but there is a strong commitment to alerting church members to the power of
television—not just the religious variety—to distort
personal and social values. This major emphasis on
education is shared in offices on other floors of the
Inter-church Center, and particularly in that of Dr
William Fore, in charge of the communications
work of the NCCC—and himself a minister of the
United Methodist Church.

Ben Logan is a broadcast producer with United
Methodist Communications. He is also the editor of
a major handbook on television awareness training
(T-A-T) entitled *The Viewer's Guide for Family and
Community*. He describes television as 'this odyssey
into the unknown for which we had no leader and
no map'. 'We can no longer play the game of inno-
cence,' he writes. 'We have only to step back, look
objectively at our relationship with television, to
know a lot about what happened when we bought
into this 20th-century pied piper that seemed to
promise so much and has left so many of us feeling
hollow.'

Much of the argument against television hinges
on its lack of reality. In his introduction to T-A-T,
Ben Logan recalls a time when there was 'a rash of
motorcycle-riding creeps on the TV screen, doing
almost exclusively things that made me angry and
afraid. They were brutal and irresponsible. Their
standard uniform was helmets, black jackets, metal
studs and hair. Now here's the problem. I have
never known a real-life, motorcyle-riding, leather-
jacket person. I lack what I call a reality check to
test my TV experience against. So when I see a
real-life motorcycle rider who fits the stereotyped

description, I am suspicious, uneasy and even frightened.'

The Viewer's Guide contains specialist articles on television news, sports, sexuality, advertising, minorities and even theology. There are also worksheets with sometimes devastating questions for small groups. For example:

> *1.* Your child asks permission to watch a show such as where there is sure to be at least one murder.

> *2.* Your child says there is going to be a real-life murder in the neighbourhood and asks permission to go and watch.
>
> *Questions:* What would you do in each case? How different are the two situations? What effect do you think each situation would have on the child? If you say yes to either request, what does this say to the child about your attitude to violence?

The United Methodists' commitment to television awareness training is important. As the biggest mainline Protestant church, they could influence the policies of other American denominations. As it is, T-A-T is the only serious alternative policy to electronic evangelism. A major criticism by Christian media educators of the Electronic Church is that it has simply 'baptised' a potentially dangerous medium. Despite the high motives of many television preachers, they proclaim their gospel from a land of illusion. There are so many illusions already in television-land. A few more of a religious variety can be fitted in just too comfortably.

This is the non-financial reason why the mainline churches cannot compete with the TV preachers. But there is another reason. Even if what William Fore describes as the 'spirit of deregulation' could be contained, or the churches could set aside sufficient funds to buy airtime on equal terms, they could still not compete. A church has what Nelson Price, director of UMCom's public media division, describes as a 'plurastic constituency'. The independent operator builds up a following of viewers

who identify with *him*. But the members of a
national church can hardly be expected to agree
on something so personal as a favourite television
preacher. By definition, a church (like its New
Testament) cannot focus on one evangelist alone.
An evangelistic association, supporting an individual preacher, can do so, and the result is almost
inevitably a cult of personality.

Nevertheless, United Methodist Communications is involved in broadcasting, and the objectives
are clear but limited. *Catch the Spirit* is a magazine
programme for cable television. It is intended for
those who are already members of the Church and
for those who might be attracted to become so.
There are two young presenters. Hilly Hicks is a
black Los Angeles actor and also a Methodist minister. Emily Simer, a blonde psychiatric social work-
er, is also an actor, and a minister's daughter. The
show is brightly produced, much of it on location.
It has a magazine format to 'explore the pluralism of
the Church'. The producers strive for 'openness'
and 'acceptance' rather than 'overt theology'.

A typical programme includes two documentary
pieces, an 'issues' section with a studio interview, a
book or film review and a comment on some aspect
of the life of the Church by Ken Briggs, former
religious editor of *The New York Times*. There are
occasional Specials with orchestras, choirs and
nationally-known soloists. The annual cost of the
weekly show is $1,200,000. A Special (*Catch the
Spirit at Christmas*) can cost as much as $60,000.
The show is broadcast on four 'networks'—CBN,
ACTS, AVN and New York's black entertainment
network. The Specials have a wider circulation; and
UMCom takes advantage of what remains open in
public interest (and therefore free) broadcasting on
the national networks. NBC and ABC each provide
approximately four hours a year. CBS is seemingly
more generous, with up to 20 half-hours; but, sadly
for Nelson Price, 'the local affiliates can chop out'.
There have been real successes on national television. Within ten days of the first news of the Ethi-
opian famine, UMCom had national television

spots appealing for money: $150,000 was collected at the Church's national headquarters, and a great deal more was handed in to local United Methodist churches.

Successes are needed on television, if for no higher reason than to satisfy the Church's own membership. There is an involvement in some broadly cultural material such as a programme on *How Children Learn*. An investment of time and money is exchanged for a mention of United Methodist Communications on the programme's list of credits. The Church participates in the work of the Protestant Radio and TV Center in Atlanta, which itself has had a 40-year involvement in American radio. UMCom has a characteristically well-defined objective in radio, and provides local churches and ministers with the *Word and Music* radio script service. It offers a 'blend of local and national materials, adaptable to any listening audience'.

The United Methodist Church covers 97 per cent of the geographical area of the United States. The Rev Elmer Gantry, a pre-United Methodist if ever there was one, progressed from the boondocks to what his bishop called 'a somewhat larger town' of 4,100. Then, after making a name for himself in his public battle against sensualists and malefactors, he was rewarded with the Wellspring Church in 'Zenith', very large and once fashionable but with problems calling for heroic endeavours. The United Methodists are not a denomination with too many megachurches, for their tight structuring militates against the highly personalised ministry that can flourish in a more congregationalist setting. There are, however, a dozen or so exceptionally large major local churches whose numerical strength has been built up over a long period.

One such is First Methodist Church, Shreveport, in the North Eastern corner of Louisiana but near the centre of the tri-state region that unpoetic locals call the Arklatex. With a facade of six tall classical columns, the church stands at the head of Texas Street in the heart of downtown Shreveport. It is an imposing, perhaps majestic, building designed and added to by latter-day admirers of Sir Christopher Wren. Under a great and very recent central spire that dominates the neighbourhood, the church is in fact a series of buildings. The sanctuary, enveloped in glowing stained glass, can seat 1,200 people. An activities building includes assembly rooms, class-rooms and lounges, a gymnasium, a rooftop swimming pool and parking garages. A three-storey education block is used by both children and adults.

This church could easily have joined in the middle-class flight from the cities. It had the financial resources and the offer of a new site. Like St Luke's Episcopal Church, Atlanta, it stayed put and has clearly won the battle against suburban religion. It has a membership of 6,000 and an annual budget of $1,700,0000. There are fifty-two staff members on the payroll, many of them working from well appointed offices that might well have been transplanted from a successful corporation. The atmosphere is businesslike but not slick. The senior minister, Dr John D. Fellers, a pipe-smoking Texan, is, like his predecessor, the much loved Dr D.L. Dykes, committed to broadcasting. Sunday morning services are broadcast on regional television, cablevision and radio. An estimated 60,000 people throughout the Arklatex have come to regard First Methodist Church, Shreveport, as in some sense their own. Dr Dykes, now senior minister emeritus, estimates that 90 per cent of new members of the church are attracted in the first instance by television. His successor cheerfully admits that in televised worship there have to be certain simplifications which he describes as 'liturgical trade-offs'.

The Sunday broadcasts, and an extensive use of television for Sunday school teacher training, are only the tip of a much greater commitment to broadcasting at First Methodist Church. In yet another building in the complex is sited a $5 million television studio and control room. On one corner of its low flat roof sits a great computer-controlled uplink antenna dish capable of accessing 17 of America's 21 broadcast satellites. This is AVN, the

Alternate View Network. It is sponsored by First Methodist Church, and its general manager, Dr Curtis Chambers, is also a member of the church's staff. Formerly he was general secretary of United Methodist Communications.

AVN represents the greatest investment yet by an American mainline congregation in satellite broadcasting and in the technology that has helped the Electronic Church to its present dominant position. For four and a quarter hours each Sunday, using the Galaxy I satellite (Transponder 22), there is a sequence of mainly half-hour programmes, including *Sunday School Live*, with a studio audience and call-in questions; *Questions of Faith*, an edited version of morning worship from First Methodist Church, interviews, discussions, a religious news update and music videos. In future, *Catch the Spirit* will be included in the schedule. AVN also carries a half-hour version of the Sunday Eucharist of the South's other radio-active mainline congregation, St Luke's Episcopal Church, Atlanta.

In satellite-to-cable broadcasting, position and timing are all-important. Hopes are high at AVN, for, on Transponder 22, it immediately precedes the Discovery Channel, 'wholesome, family entertainment' with a growing reputation for programmes about science, technology, nature, history, travel and adventure programming.

Hi-tech broadcasting is expensive. In 1985, AVN spent $135,000 on its satellite lease. Of the recent mainline initiatives in broadcasting—and there have been very few—AVN stands the best chance of success. Describing itself as 'the real alternative', the enterprise has attracted some major donations. It is undergirded by one of the largest and most active congregations in the United Methodist Church. Curtis Chambers is a professional and has held appointments at the centre of his own denomination and also with the NCCC and WACC. The central task is to persuade cable operators to take AVN so that it may indeed become a network in more than name. Personal visits are being made to multiple system owners throughout the Arklatex. Dr D.L.

Dykes has been further afield, preaching the word to system owners in Colorado, where cablevision began ('because of the mountains').

AVN is also a commercial undertaking, and is licensed by the FCC as a private carrier. The four major national networks make regular use of the up-link facility for news feeds. In a memorable 'two-hop' broadcast, battling Jesse Jackson, sitting in Shreveport, confronted South African journalists in Johannesburg. National star Terry Bradshaw, former quarter-back with the Pittsburg Steelers, is a regular visitor to the studios. During the season— all the way from Louisiana—he is football critic for his hometown's KDKA TV. His punchy comments travel 66,000 kilometres through space before reaching Pennsylvania. This is one of AVN's regular commercial assignments and has nothing to do with religion. It is entirely coincidental that, all those years before, on KDKA Radio, the first religious service was broadcast from Pittsburg's Calvary Episcopal Church. That too may have had little to do with religion. It was arranged more as a technical feat than as a spiritual exercise, and the rector was too busy to take part. AVN just might become a national vehicle for mainline ministers with different priorities.

Chapter 10

A chapter of Acts

'About midnight Paul and Silas were praying and singing hymns to God, and the other prisoners were listening to them.'—Acts of the Apostles, Chapter 16, verse 25.

Before the American invasion, few outsiders worried much about Grenada. Leon Edwards was a prisoner on the island, not for his political convictions but for murder. One night he had a drunken quarrel over a woman. It ended after he had slashed his opponent to death. He spent two years on death row before his sentence was commuted to life imprisonment. He was not a model prisoner, and spent many weeks in solitary confinement. One night, he was listening to the radio in his cell and heard the *Baptist Hour*. He sent for the free Bible study material; and this began a long correspondence with J.P. Allen, then head of the counselling department of the Southern Baptists' Radio and Television Commission.

Leon Edwards' story is not a long one. He became a Christian and also the natural leader of a group of fellow believers in prison. J.P. Allen visited Grenada with a film crew to produce a documentary on this man who had such a deep influence on everyone who met him. During this visit, Leon Edwards was baptised. One evening he took part as usual in the prison service and sang with the prison trio. During the night he died—quietly and of natural causes. It was a few weeks before his 33rd birthday. If he had lived 130 years earlier, he might have found his Grenadian jailors less sympathetic. Also, as a black West Indian, he might have been

less attracted to the Southern Baptist message and
indeed to the other Southern churches.

★   ★   ★   ★   ★

It is the world's largest evangelical denomination.
In the stressful years that led up to the war for
Southern independence, it separated itself from the
agency that was the focus for denominational unity.
Much that was Southern has now gone with the
wind; but not so the Southern Baptist Convention.
It has multiplied. There are now almost 14 million
members in every state of the union. Unlike the
other churches of the Confederacy, their split with
their Northern co-religionists has never been re-
paired. Indeed, the schism occurred years before
the outbreak of war. Slavery, of course, has long
since ceased to be a cause of division. Today there
are new differences. The issue remains one of conservatism. The social conservatism that could lead
Southern Christians to tolerate and even defend
slavery has been overthrown, but a biblical conservatism flourishes that has given the Southern
Baptists a special missionary zeal and taken them to
96 countries of the world.

Despite its regard for the independence of each
local congregation, the Southern Baptist Convention is also a developed denomination. Soon after it
was created, its founding fathers could speak in a
surprisingly non-independent tone of their 'church'
rather than their 'churches'. The three mighty central agencies of the SBC are the Sunday school
board and the boards for home and foreign mis-
sions. The broadcasting arm of the Church is the
Radio and Television Commission which, since
1955, has been based in Fort Worth, Texas, but
which (interestingly) has its roots in Shreveport,
Louisiana, and Atlanta, Georgia.

The commission's first headquarters was in
Atlanta. Its early flagship programme was *The
Baptist Hour*. The very first speaker was Dr M.E.
Dodd, Pastor of First Baptist Church, Shreveport;
and his message, delivered from his church, just 11
months before Pearl Harbour, was 'Christ and Hu-

man Crises'. The programme was heard on 17 radio stations in 11 states. Today the commission's programmes are seen and heard more than 6,000 times a week on more than 4,000 radio and television stations. The commision claims to be the world's largest producer of non-sectarian, inspirational programmes for radio. The current television output includes *The Athletes*, in which sports personalities talk about their faith; *JOT*, about an animated cartoon character who teaches children about God; and a drama/documentary series, *The Human Dimension*. Then there is the continuing legacy from the heyday of public service religious broadcasting. The commission consults with ABC, CBS and NBC over the production of occasional special PBS programmes. In 1979, Dr Jimmy P. Allen, a former President of the Southern Baptist Convention, and the man who baptised Leon Edwards, became president of the Radio and Television Commission.

Southern Baptists are not part of the ecumenical, central, mainline group of Protestant churches. They declined to join the Federal Council of Churches (FCCC). They see themselves as evangelicals, and they have never lost their embattled pre-Civil War sense of separateness. Nevertheless, they are better organised and more co-ordinated than the churches which look to bishops for leadership. The powerful boards of the Southern Baptists are not just central agencies of the Church. Theirs is a complicated, anomalous story. The Church created the boards and the boards created the Church.

In recent years there has been a split in the Southern Baptists between fundamentalists and moderate conservatives. They present two images to America. On the one hand they are a mildly isolationist but well organised and successful denomination. They now far outnumber all other Baptists put together. The other image is of a parent of a family of highly independent and sometimes eccentric preaching stars. Billy Graham and Jerry Falwell are Baptists. So is Pat Robertson, albeit of a charismatic variety. Dr Charles F. Stanley somehow bridges the organisational/entrepreneurial divide. He is a former

president of the Convention, but he is also an independent electronic evangelist in his own right.

This all means that the denomination has a
slightly schizophrenic approach to the Electronic
Church. As well as the evangelical superstars,
many lesser-known ministers and churches are
involved in buying time on local television and
cablevision. However, the Radio and Television
Commission, in its official pronouncements on
the financing of evangelism, sounds almost like a
member of the National Council of Churches. It
agrees that 'many people in both secular and religious communities are offended by the often sen-
sational religionists of today who continually ask
for money'. Unlike the mainline communicators,
Southern Baptists certainly see broadcasting as an
evangelistic tool. In a bright demonstration video
introduced by David Soul, they claim, there is 'in a
hi-tech world, a hi-tech answer—Jesus Christ'.
They assert (with the Electronic Church) an evangelical urgency to fulfil the great commission to
preach the Gospel to every nation. But denomina-
tionally they have set their face against fund-raising
on air. For similar reasons, they make no attempt to
create their own home-grown Baptist media stars.
Instead, they believe they can tap the Church's
enormous numerical and ideological strength and
thus compete—they would not use the word—in
broadcasting.

By any standard, the commission is a big operation. Twenty-nine different radio and television
programmes are produced and distributed on a
weekly basis. The most talked-about aspect of the
work is also the most recent. In August 1981, the
commission signed a contract for its own satellite
transponder. This was the first step in launching
ACTS—the American Christian Television System—the Southern Baptists' own network and the
first *denominational* attempt to provide a national
television service. The attempt is faltering. The
financial foundations on which the Electronic
Church is built remain as solid as ever. The starkly
simple argument for viewer-sustained, bought-time

religious television remains unchallenged.

As with the mainline churches, the Southern Baptists found it increasingly difficult to obtain non-commercial airtime. Meanwhile an independent Southern Baptist, Billy Graham, could film a three-night crusade in Seattle or another major city, edit down to three one-hour programmes and buy time on several hundred stations—all paid for by the offerings of the viewer. Under the presidency of Dr Jimmy Allen, the Radio and Television Commission saw a new opening in religious broadcasting when the Federal Communications Commission began to consider low-power television—'the first new broadcasting service the agency had proposed in 20 years'. The new low-power UHF stations would have a range of up to 15 miles and they would provide a new layer in American broadcasting. In 1980 and 1981, the Southern Baptists applied for licences for 125 low-power stations. ACTS was created as a non-profit corporation to apply for LPTV licences and if possible to do so in the name of a local church.

The new tier of television stations provided the impetus for ACTS, but it was also proposed to carry programming on full-power television and, of course, on cable systems. Here indeed could be a real network. Time-buying could be avoided and in the only way possible—by station-buying. The system would allow for local broadcasting. Three and a half million dollars' worth of programmes were already stockpiled at the commission's Forth Worth headquarters. The whole system would be tied together by satellite. A transponder on Spacenet 1 was chosen. It had been launched by the European Ariane rocket. Its footprint includes the Caribbean, Canada and Mexico. This same satellite is used by the Southern Baptists' Home Mission Board (BTN) for internal educational and training work.

The Church was confident—too confident—that ACTS affiliates would readily install the necessary receiving equipment. Applications for low-power TV stations soon got out of hand. There were 6,750, and the FCC declared it would have to rethink. By 1985, ACTS had acquired licences for only five LPTV stations including one in Hawaii and another in Alaska. This failure forced a change of direction. For the immediate future, the main thrust would have to be towards cable systems.

ACTS is designed to offer 'quality, alternative programming with diverse audience appeal'. The network ought to have a broad base. There are 36,000 local churches, 72 Baptist-supported colleges and universities and 3,000 missionaries. The local Baptist Church is the 'key to its philosophy' but it is also proving to be a lock that will not open for ACTS. The concept is revolutionary but simple and would seem to dovetail into the Baptist ideal of local responsibility. The hope remains that a Southern Baptist Church in any part of the United States will buy from the denomination a package of TVRO receiving equipment and, if it wishes, a supplementary package of TV cameras for simple local input. The Church will become a recognised ACTS Cable Affiliate (ACCA) and feed the ACTS network —and locally generated material—into its neighbourhood cable system. The agreement of the cable operator is, of course, all-important.

The commission provides a great deal of guidance about the most sensitive way to approach a cable company. The initial move should be made by a group of local business people. Much is made of the fact that ACTS transmits some of the programming of the mainline churches. This undoubtedly carries weight with cable operators; but it is a two-edged sword. Too much emphasis on ecumenism switches off the network's grassroots Baptist supporters. 'Strong-arming'—when a local church organises a telephone lobby to urge a cable operator to carry a particular programme—often has catastrophic results for the lobbyists. They are often revealed to be uninformed about the cause for which they are lobbying. Small cable operators have a limited number of telephone lines and resent having their time wasted. ACTS does offer some carrots to the operator, including 224 (30-second) spot announcements for his exclusive use.

For ACTS, the problems are piling up. The network is costing $10 million a year, and it seems that half of that figure is coming as a direct subsidy from the denomination. It had been hoped to sell national as well as local advertising. This will only become attractive to national advertisers if the potential audience reaches 12 to 15 million viewers. At present it stands at about three million. Local churches that are cable affiliates pay eight cents per member per month for the satellite feed.

Some church members feel they already support the denomination through a voluntary quota payment, and cannot understand why this should have to be supplemented. The response from the local congregations has been disappointing. About $60,000 a month is subscribed. Some of the most active ministers and congregations are already heavily involved in their own broadcasting. The mood in the Fort Worth headquarters is downbeat but determined. The denomination has given permission for ACTS to mount a major fund-raising campaign, and the hope is that after three years things will improve and there will be sufficient audience build-up. The number of employees has been cut from a peak of 176, in May 1984, to a barely sufficient 97.

This $25 million enterprise deserves to succeed. It is by far the biggest and bravest attempt by an American church to undo the effects of broadcast deregulation. In its Sunday schedules, ACTS plays fair with the other denominations which use the network. The choice of Spacenet 1 has caused no problems and, of course, fits well with the Church's internal use of satellite technology. It might have caused consumer resistance if ACTS had been intended for direct transmission to cable companies already locked on different satellites. But that is not the intention. ACTS is different, and its route to the screens of America is different. In fact there are two main routes. The first, via low-power TV, is blocked at the moment. The second is to the local church first and then on to the cable system.

In an ideal world this novel delivery system

would work brilliantly. Local congregations would realise their part in a grand design that would for the first time provide an alternative to the Electronic Church. But they do not realise that the stakes are so high, and they might not approve if they did. Many of them enjoy the TV preachers, for in many cases the theological distance is not great. In the meantime, ACTS and its Texas apostles reaffirm their 'no solicitation policy' that is absolutely revolutionary but somehow does not sound so. 'ACTS,' say the glossy handouts, 'is a refreshing alternative to full-time religious network programming. ACTS refuses to solicit funds in order to raise money for the network. We will not compromise our viewers' standards, nor our reputation, by asking for money.' The problem is that the viewer and the church member do not appreciate these high standards.

Chapter 11

Numbers game

In a local church, the empty pew cannot lie. Church attendance statistics are available Sunday by Sunday. Figures for baptisms and communions can easily be computed. Most decisive of all, the parish treasurer, even if he stays at home for a whole Sunday, will know instantly how the wind is blowing. But the religious broadcaster can lie easily and boldly. In fact, everything conspires to assist him not to tell the truth. What kind of person would admit that no-one much is listening to him? Religious broadcasters mostly believe in God. All of them just have to believe in the audience. Prayer to oneself may be possible. Broadcasting most certainly is not.

From the beginning of religious broadcasting there has been an uncontrollable tendency to exaggerate numbers. It has been so easy to 'think of a number and double it'. One televangelist once claimed an audience of 100 million, but then changed his tune to a more modest '1.4 million weekly'. Another was accused by the Television Information Office of multiplying his real audience figures by a factor of 60! Another's claim for 20 million viewers was described by his associates in his hometown paper as a 'total fabrication'. Religious broadcasters generally have probably been the worst offenders in the entire industry. A purveyor of pop music, weather forecasts or nature programmes can be relatively detached about his product. He is not trying to change the world. The electronic churchman is trying to do just that. He cannot admit that he is less popular than he was. Tomorrow always has to be better than today. Everything has to be 'up-up-up'.

These are the stars that can never set. Their Lord can be crucified by poor ratings, but they need success. God is continually doing 'mighty things' for their broadcasting ministries. This, of course, is easily identified as the old one-more-heave-and-we've-made-it revivalism. Radio and television have accentuated the tendency to claim continual success. The televangelists not only have to sound good, they have to look good. They are conformed to the world of their audience. John the Baptist would not be allowed in front of their cameras until he had had his hair cut and been fitted out with a sober suit and the regulation floppy leather Bible. He would probably soon become 'Dr John'.

In most areas of public broadcasting there has to be some attempt to assess audience size. The American Electronic Church has largely escaped this indignity because it has developed as a unique state-within-a-state. The new religious broadcasting is different from secular broadcasting, not just because it is religious but because it stands on a new and novel economic basis. It is paid for, using other people's money, by the broadcaster himself. He does not have to produce audience figures for his sponsor. Generally he has no advertisers to satisfy. He needs an audience to impress and to preserve his cash flow. He can, if he chooses, pull an audience figure out of the air and declare it as gospel.

The religious broadcaster is aided and abetted in all this by the new realities of satellite-to-cable television. A subscriber to a cable system will have access to 30, 40, 50 and even more separate channels. If a televangelist has a slot on one of those channels, he can claim all kinds of things about his relationship with that subscriber. This preacher is on a satellite. His footprint is stamped across a great country. He *could* be seen or heard by millions. Everything tempts him to assume that this is in fact happening and that—through God's blessing—he is a star.

The science of audience measurement is in any case exceedingly complicated. A great variety of questions have to be asked and answered. The only way to get at the real facts would be to ask everyone who watches television to talk about themselves and their precise viewing habits. Audiences can only be estimated, and this is done by asking questions of a few people who hopefully represent the rest. A direct question—'Do you watch the Richard Roberts Show?'—has to be backed up with further enquiries: 'For how long each day?'; 'How old are you?'; 'Where do you live?'—and so on. A bald statement—'X million Americans watch Elmer Gantry'—is almost meaningless until it has been filled out with further information. Then, of course, audience measurement is not simply a matter of counting heads. It is all-important to know who is watching and listening; and, in the case of religious broadcasting, to know if a programme appeals to the old or the young, or to those who are active members of local churches, or to outsiders hitherto untouched by religion. If it can be proved that the Electronic Church is mainly viewed by evangelicals, it would have to be understood as an agency for confirming religious beliefs and conferring status on believers. Audience measurement should also indicate whether the Electronic Church is a distraction from local church involvement or if, on the other hand, it supports and undergirds the life of local congregations.

In answering all these questions, it would be a great help to know how many Americans are in fact content to think of themselves as 'evangelicals'. Estimates vary between 20 and 60 million! If to be evangelical means to support the political programme of new-right groupings like the Liberty Federation, then there are probably 'only' 12 to 15 million. In other words, no-one really knows. From the Southern Baptists outwards (or inwards, depending on your point of view) there is such a gradation of belief that ultimately evangelical may be a term without much meaning. Within the Electronic Church it covers a multitude of sins (or virtues) and brackets together such diverse theologies as those of Evangelist Swaggart and Dr Schuller.

The opposing camp is not above putting around a

few well chosen numerical notions. It is claimed
that the NBC, CBS and ABC special programmes
for Christmas and Easter have a greater audience
than the programmes of the Electronic Church.
Taking on the televangelists one at a time, Dr William Fore concluded in 1982 that 'while the purchase of time by syndicated TV evangelists has drast-
ically reduced the number of stations carrying the
mainline network programming, the aggregate audience for these mainline programmes, taken as a
whole, is still considerably greater than the largest
syndicated evangelist'. National Religious Broadcasters claim 85 per cent of all religious programming is by their own members. For once, many
mainliners would see this figure as a wild *under*-
estimate.

There has been long-term disagreement over the
meaning of the available statistics. This has been
partly—and only partly—allayed by a research report by the University of Pennsylvania's Annenberg
School of Communications and the Gallup Organisation. The Annenberg report was funded by
an ad hoc committee representing the National
Council of Churches, the US Catholic Conference,
National Religious Broadcasters, CBN, PTL, *Old
Time Gospel Hour*, the Southern Baptist Sunday
School Board and 32 other organisations. The study
cost $175,000, with CBN making the biggest single
donation. As well as analysing the content of religious programmes, the researchers made a national
and two regional surveys of viewers of religious and
other programmes.

Among many different findings, the investigators
found that in both religious and prime-time television programmes those at either end of the life cycle
are strikingly under-represented, and blue-collar
workers, the unemployed, the retired and house-
wives are almost invisible. Catholics rarely appear
on the screen. The report estimated that, corrected
for duplication, the American religious television
audience, watching for at least 15 minutes weekly,
stands at 13.3 million—or about 6 per cent of the
national television audience. The researchers did

not find evidence to suggest that cable has had a major effect on religious viewing.

Fourteen per cent of viewers claimed that religious programmes were a substitute for church attendance. Among those who do not watch religious television, 71 per cent said they would change the channel if a religious programme appeared. Viewers of religious material tended to be less educated, lower-income, female, older and non-white. Overall, religious programming, whether by mainline churches or independent ministries, serves primarily to reinforce the religious beliefs of the viewers.

The Annenberg report had a somewhat dampening effect on the confidence of the backroom boys of the Electronic Church. Some of them discount the findings and are critical of its consideration of cable. There is not a great deal in the report to uplift the mainline broadcasters, but at least it puts the televangelists in their place.

But the TV preachers sense that, in fact, they have a very large audience. The main indication continues to come from the telephone. CBN now expects four million calls a year. It has now surpassed American Airlines as the largest single user of the toll-free 800 service (the equivalent of Britain's Freefone).

Within 18 months the hearts of evangelical statisticians began to lift. They had been right all the time, or so they believe. The two leading audience rating firms are Arbitron and the A.C. Nielsen Company. According to a new survey conducted by Nielsen, 61 million people watched one or more of the top ten syndicated religious programmes during February 1985. Each week during that month, 21.1 per cent of all television households watched at least six minutes of these programmes. When the whole of February is considered as a single entity, the viewing figure reaches 40.1 per cent.

The traditional method of estimating ratings is to organise a sample of about 500 households in most of the 200 or so American television markets (see Glossary). Each household is provided with a diary.

At the end of a four-week period, these are collected together to become the basic data for arriving at local and national rating estimates.

Nielsen has developed an automated audience measurement system. 1,700 households are selected nationwide. Every TV set in each home is wired to a recording device which remembers precisely how that set has been used. In the middle of the night, information is fed by telephone to a central computer. The data thus produced is known as the Nielsen Television Index (NTI). It is not foolproof. Nielsen is only aware that a TV set is switched on to a channel—not whether it is actually being looked at. By combining the findings of NTI with NHI (Nielsen Homevideo Index), which rates commercial cable networks, it has been demonstrated that during this vital month of February 1985 the *The 700 Club* was seen in a total of 16.3 million homes. The total number of daily viewers was 4.5 million (unduplicated).

In the numbers game, it is now 40–30 to the evangelicals ... with the mainliners to serve.

Chapter 12

Some as big as your head

NASA's Goddard Space Flight Center has a hybrid look about it, part university campus and part industrial zone. It has helped itself to a generous slice of gentle Maryland. Here and there among its widely dispersed structures are one or two concessions to public curiosity. There is a small building in which radio hams can play the satellites. There is also a glass-sided exhibition hall, much humbler than the great air and space museum in Washington, but nevertheless an American Pantheon. In this hall, no bigger than a car saleroom, stands a congested crowd of little tin gods that can fly high around our world and have changed our lives by upsetting our boundaries.

The fundamentalists' dismissiveness of 'evolutionary nonsense' seems particularly appropriate at Goddard. Among the satellite species there seems to be a total absence of any principle of family resemblance. After all, Patagonian parents usually produce Patagonian children. Aeroplanes, whether they have open cockpits or delta wings, are easily identified as aeroplanes. But every member of the satellite family is an uninhibited and exotic individualist. One junior member of the family is really nothing more than a shiny football trailing a spindly plumage of aerials. Another is a simple drum, covered from head to foot with a thousand reflecting facets. If only this fellow had been made spherical like his cousin, he could have spent his retirement on a ballroom ceiling throwing speckles of colour over dancers in the dark. Standing next to him is a dreary and sullen creature. He is vulnerable. He needs to be moved only a few feet and he could

● *High-flying 'angel':*
Intelsat

easily be mistaken for the exhibition's trash can. Further along the line stands a gleaming alloy porcupine who would probably do rather well for himself in a museum of contemporary art. That nasty bit of work over there looks just like one of those skull-cracking iron balls that battling bishops used to whirl around their armour-plated tonsures. They were prevented by their religion from drawing their swords!

Satellites come in all shapes and sizes. Some have been smaller than a pumpkin; others will soon be as big as a bus. Many could never be put on public display. These are the secret angels, equipped with all-seeing eyes. During the Falklands conflict, a Soviet spy satellite was brought into such low orbit over the South Atlantic fleet that it survived for only five earth orbits. But before burning up, its camera would have read any uncamouflaged markings on vehicles parked on the decks of the British ships. Angels of light, fortunately still on the drawing board, will one day be able to smite their foes with deadly laser beams. Then there are the angels of peace—or profit, at least. Their tasks are weather forecasting, telephone communications, ship navigation, astronomy, measurement of continental drift and surveying the earth's resources.

Not everyone sees satellites as angels. The French SPOT, launched in February 1986, is in a

North-South polar orbit and is capable of identify-
ing everything on earth that is more than 30ft long.
An enormous amount of commercial and military
knowledge about every single nation is available
from its knowledge gained for profit and without
permission. Third World protests at the UN have
been to no avail.

In broadcasting, too, satellites pose new threats.
It will be increasingly difficult to regulate commercial advertising. In Britain, some politicians fear
that election broadcasting, so carefully regulated by
the Representation of the People Act, may suffer
partisan intrusions from high in the sky.

Evangelicals have few doubts about satellites;
even the military variety. The Strategic Defense Initiative ('Star Wars') was, after all, itself the initiative of the President whom evangelicals supported
overwhelmingly in two elections. As for satellite
broadcasting, it has been a decisive factor in the
success of their Electronic Church. Every preacher
with the capacity to uplink his gospel can see it return a hundredfold in a beam that *could* be picked
up just about anywhere in the country. Whether his
seed falls upon stony ground or not is not so vitally
important as the preacher's own response to the
great commission to preach the gospel to every creature. At long last the parable of the sower can come
true. He that has ears to hear, let him buy a dish.

The notion that the satellites that carry American
entertainment television really might be angelic
beings foretold in the Apocalypse is put about widely within the Electronic Church. At close quarters
there is not much that is gossamer-like about these
creations. In fact, they are ugly brutes. But that is
not important. They are up there in the sky, some
of them with wings. They are invisible but real.
They do not actually 'fly' but then only pantomime
angels do that. They are accessible. Indeed, they are
cheerful capitalists, and it is simplicity itself to rent
a piece of them. Best of all, they confer status on
anyone who has the slightest dealings with them.
The evangelist with a satellite ministry is immediately made larger than life. 'Bouncing Billy'

sing the headlines, less concerned with what Dr Graham says than the technology he uses in saying it. There is a new breed of religious name-dropper. He has not actually met Gabriel or Michael, but he does know about Anik, Aurora, Telstar and Westar.

In satellite religion, the medium authenticates the message. This is not only true for the religious broadcasting that sits so happily within American entertainment television. It is also true of certain worldwide evangelical ministries that have been blown, by the communications explosion, through a side-entrance and into the chancel of the Electronic Church.

Some years have passed since 17,000 evangelical Christians crowded into the Tarrant County Convention Centre in Fort Worth, Texas, for a communion service which, with the help of eight satellites and 360 downlinks in 13 countries, included more than half a million Christians. This was the initiative of televangelist Kenneth Copeland with South Korea's mega-minister, Dr Paul Yonngi-Cho. It was the beginning of an international use of satellites by evangelicals that gets more spectacular every year. One space epic was called, appropriately, *Explo*; and it was billed as the greatest satellite show on earth—bigger than the Olympics or Live Aid. On the last five days of 1985 more than 600,000 people gathered at 100 different conference centres in every continent. For two hours each day they were linked together on huge colour television screens. The link-up was made possible by 18 communications satellites. This biggest-ever global teleconference was sponsored by Campus Crusade for Christ, Dr Bill Bright's California-based Christian training ministry. The conference opened in Seoul, Korea. At the end of each broadcast, Bill Bright and his fellow leaders flew off to another major conference centre. Contributors to *Explo* included Billy Graham, Luis Palau and Bishop Festo Kivengere.

Campus Crusade estimated that the cost of a one-site student conference could have been $2,000 per participant. Satellite tele-conferencing reduced ex-

● *Global conference sponsor Bill Bright*

penses to $40 per person. British Telecom International had won the contract to conduct the biggest-ever orchestra of satellites. The worldwide centre of operations was in the Limehouse Studios in London's Dockland. Inevitably technological difficulties forced compromises on the programme's organisers. Sometimes the pace slowed as Nairobi crossed to California, or Manila came in with an observation. Sometimes, too, there were hitches as one or other of the 50 simultaneous translation services was lost. But the atmosphere in Limehouse was electric as fast-talking New Yorkers conferred with cool Telecom engineers and the born-again shouted, ever-hopefully: 'Harare—where are you?'

Each day the two-hour programme ended with a time of prayer. Koreans, Filipinos, Icelanders, Dutchmen, Argentinians and Cambodians followed one another on to the screen. Their heads were sometimes bowed in prayer—the same prayer—despite distances of many thousands of miles. Then, in an awesome display of synchronisation, all 600,000 participants, in their village churches and splendid conference centres, sang the conference theme song, 'Come, Help Change the World'.

Certainly satellites are changing the world. Stripped of the shameless angelic hype, they are simply a means for putting angles (not angels!) in microwaves. It is these angles that mean the world will never be the same again. Worldwide television is now a possibility.

Satellites are also changing evangelicals. The electronic tentacles of the huge closed-circuit tele-conferences are giving those who participate a self-confidence, a discipline and a sense of belonging to a worldwide institution that up to now only the centrally-structured churches have enjoyed. Delighted with the 'overwhelming' response to *Explo 85*, Bill Bright has announced an even bigger event for 1990.

These new forms of inter-Christian communications are not 'broadcasting' at all. Many churches, punch drunk from the fundamentalist bombardment from outer space, have failed to grasp the importance of satellite tele-conferencing. However, American Catholics and Southern Baptists do have in place their own internal satellite networks (CTNA and BTN). The Paulist National Catholic Evangelistic Association is planning a $500,000, eight-hour national tele-conference. The local gatherings will take place in the USA's Holiday Inns, and Catholics will make use of the hotel chain's existing satellite network.

But the churches of the world are far behind the independent evangelicals in exploiting satellite communications. There is no sign yet of the international initiatives that have become such a part of the evangelicals' armoury.

Perhaps this will always be so. Perhaps Marconi, hard at work building a brand new transmitter for the Pope, was just a flash in the pan. Perhaps religious broadcasting, and even religious narrow-casting, is destined to be dominated by independent, swashbuckling entrepreneurs. Perhaps only stars can shine on television. Perhaps there is some intrinsic problem with churches that stifles initiative and snuffs out the bright lights. This would be disappointment enough. What would be really catastrophic would be a verdict that the traditional churches are in fact tongue-tied; that they could really afford the hardware but they have nothing much to say to the world or even to each other. Is television-land really so wicked that the best the churches can do is to warn people about its seductive charms?

Chapter 13

Priests and Profits

The United States of America is probably the only country on earth where a new church building can be the cause of a bitter zoning dispute. Suburban activists have been known to reach high levels of excitement over the increase of road traffic caused by Christians! Nowhere else in the Western world could sheer numbers of churchgoers be conceivably regarded as an environmental hazard. The Christian religion flourishes in North America. People attend Sunday worship in great numbers.

The overwhelming majority of these Sunday (and indeed midweek) worshippers belong to the traditional churches. Most belong to the mainline Protestant denominations that had their roots in Europe. One in three is a Roman Catholic.

But when it comes to broadcasting, which in so many powerful ways influences the values and defines the culture of the modern state, the traditional American churches are almost silent and almost invisible.

The evangelical broadcasters' argument is that the old faiths are played out or that they have nothing worthwhile to say. On the airwaves of America they are now tongue-tied and this is no doubt part of the justice of God. Liberal Protestantism has had its day and has been found wanting. As for Roman Catholics, they are too numerous for a direct frontal assault and, more important still, they are a too valuable and cohesive fraction of the televangelists' donor base.

The interesting thing about Catholics is that so many of them are temperamentally prepared for the certitudes of televised religion. Accordingly, there is an unspoken understanding between the TV

Preacher and the Roman quarter of his congregation. Attacks on 'liberals' are allowed. They are the common enemy. But the papacy and the doctrines of the Assumption and the Immaculate Conception are off-limits. They are neither mocked nor condemned — nor mentioned.

The Bible is presented as the common ground of Christendom. Biblical interpretation is fundamentalist. The teaching of the televangelists about Armageddon, the end of the world, and the State of Israel would hardly earn the imprimatur of any Vatican Biblical Commission. But it is *the Bible* that the preacher is holding up to the camera. He has to be legitimate, for the Bible is a Catholic book, isn't it?

Then, of course, there are some well-trodden (and almost official) footbridges linking fundamentalist and Catholic Christians. The Charismatic movement provides the most important link and allows a Father Bertolucci to have a foot in both camps. He can pound his Bible with the fervour of an Oral Roberts. 'Believe the Word' is the cry of the new, charismatic Catholic. The tiresome but once-important concern about whether or not 'The Word' should or should not contain the Apocryphal Books are now forgotten (but not by Oral Roberts).

Religious broadcasting in the United States is now firmly in the hands of independent fundamentalist preachers. The only possible counterbalance could have been provided by North American Catholicism. But, in religious broadcasting, the country's fifty-three-million-strong Catholic population is either neutralised or collaborating with the occupying power.

The traditional Protestant churches have different problems but the result is the same. They too are in internal exile from their country's airwaves. Counted together, they are twice as numerous as the mighty U.S. Catholic Church, and yet a visitor from outer space who dial-flips his television set could be forgiven for doubting their existence.

This near-total banishment of the mainline and Catholic is a relatively recent phenomenon. It has nothing to do with an evangelical tide that is supposedly sweeping America and washing away all non-evangelical impurities. Nowadays, born-again Christians may be on the crest of a modest wave but their success in capturing the religious broadcasting market place is not an ideological success. It is the straightforward, simple, and inevitable result of governmental decisions to turn broadcasting into a free-for-all market place. By handing over religious broadcasting to the highest bidder, the F.C.C. guaranteed the pre-eminence of National Religious Broadcasters, which is first and foremost a trade association of those capable of buying airtime.

American religious broadcasting has an honourable history — and a long one. It began almost with broadcasting itself. KDKA Pittsburg carried Anglican Evensong in 1921. Within twelve months, in Nebraska, the first interdenominational church service was broadcast. Two more years and the country had the first of many specifically Christian radio stations.

Unsurprisingly, in view of its size and free enterprise spirit, the United States did not develop a national broadcasting system on the transatlantic model. National radio services were eventually provided when, through a process of coalescence and empire building, three coast-to-coast networks emerged (N.B.C. and C.B.S., and later A.B.C.). But broadcasting was always commercial broadcasting. The public interest was protected and the excesses of the market place were checked by regulations laid down by the Federal government.

The king-pin in the relationship between the American churches and the broadcasting companies was the government requirement that free airtime should be provided for religious broadcasting. This requirement, enforced for several decades, resulted in the warm and mutually profitable relationship that Dr. Ben Armstrong of N.R.B. has called the 'sweetheart deal'.

Of course, it is possible to both approve and condemn the deal. Churchmen might well argue that, given the immense numerical strength of the U.S. churches, it is only right and proper that the faith and indeed culture of the nation should be given free airtime. On the other side of the argument stand those who were frustrated by the broad, objective, polite, inclusive, ecumenical nature of public service broadcasting. He who pays the piper calls the tune and, when no one is paying, the tune lacks clarity and certainty.

The 'sweetheart deal' had two effects. For many years it cushioned most of the traditional American churches from the realities of broadcasting economics. They tended to regard their easy access to radio and television as a constitutional right. On the other hand and with some justice, the Evangelicals felt themselves to be excluded.

Evangelicals had seen the 'new broadcasting technology as an exciting new means to preach the good news to every creature. The radio antenna was simply an extension of the church pulpit, a means of reaching more and more people. Evangelicals pride themselves on 'having something to say' and there is no doubt at all that, of all the Christian groups, they are able to adapt most readily to the techniques of broadcasting.

But the problem with Christian broadcasting of any kind is that it is, by definition, self-contradictory. Even the expression 'Christian broadcasting' strikes at the heart of the central Christian belief that 'the word became flesh'.

It could be said that Christian broadcasting, whether on radio or television or by Catholic, liberal, or fundamentalist, is simply one more compromise of the Incarnation.

Some would hold that Christian broadcasting is simply a contradiction in terms. Others, such as Colin Morris, 'will persist with the business of trying to do the impossible' for the simple reason that it is only through TV sets and radio receivers that millions of human beings will ever hear anything remotely like the Christian Gospel. On the airwaves, the Word certainly does not become flesh and dwell among us.

Evangelical broadcasters are themselves aware of too much reliance on the disembodied word. The search is on for 'inter-active broadcasting' and for audience response. Many different techniques have been tried. Oral Roberts or Pat Robertson feel moved to pronounce God's direct intervention on the health of a viewer in Albuquerque or Atlanta. Campus Crusade for Christ, using the new technology, has linked together one hundred different satellite downlinks in five continents. Whirring, million-dollar word processors, while not quite able to make the Word into real flesh, are at least able to present the televangelist as a personable and caring correspondent.

Evangelicals are better broadcasters than Catholics or liberal Protestants. They can present a straightforward, cut and dried message that is easily adapted to an information, entertainment, and advertising medium. But the evangelicals' near-monopoly of American religious broadcasting owes very little to the popularity or simplicity of their message.

More than anything else, evangelicals owe their present position of dominance to one act of government de-regulation: namely, that a broadcasting company that now decides to accept payment for a religious broadcast will still be seen to satisfy the time honoured requirements on public service. And so — one disarmingly simple memorandum from the F.C.C. has been able to transform (some would say disfigure) the most visible image of American religion. The 'sweetheart deal' has been sunk without trace. Religious broadcasting in now restricted to those who are able to buy airtime. The airtime buyers of the N.R.B. continue to prosper.

But why do evangelicals prosper behind microphones and cameras? Why are Catholics and mainline Protestants the new outsiders in religious broadcasting?

Evangelicals are able to raise the huge sums of money that are needed to buy time, not because of the clarity or excellence of their message, but simply because their lack of structure and constraints allows them to act as business entrepreneurs.

American revivalist preachers (as they have always been — or at least for three hundred years) are first and foremost individualists. They do not owe their pulpit to any Bishop or Board of Deacons. In the beginning was the preacher. The congregation came on the Second Day. In the Thirteen Colonies and on the Western frontier, ecclesiastical structures arrived very late on the eighth day—if at all.

The preacher is the leader and the decision maker. In twentieth-century media terms, he is the star. His is a highly-personalized ministry; hence the contortions of so many of the televangelists as they seek to hand over their earthly ministries to their natural rather than their spiritual heirs.

The campfire tub thumper of the old West was financed by his audience. Only the fittest or the sincerest or the noisiest survived. In the same way, the televangelist is sustained by a scattered group of prayer partners which is simply and by any other name—his fan club.

The independent preacher can pass round the hat at the end of the camp meeting in order to defray the necessary expenses. So can his great-grandson, the televangelist. But the churchman finds it much more difficult to function as a fast-moving entrepreneur. To begin with, he is held in position in the ecclesiastical firmament by the role conferred on him by his church.

Like the Israelites before them, Americans are pointed to God by both 'priests' and 'prophets'. 'Prophets' mark themselves out by their own vision and charisma and drive. But 'Priests' are anointed by the collective will of their church. As a general rule, they are unlikely to succeed as self-financing stars in the highly personalized and commercialized world of showbiz religion.

Glossary

Some of the acronyms, abbreviations and expressions in this list are fully explained in the preceding chapters. They are relisted here for clarity and comparison.

ACCA   ACTS CHURCH CABLE AFFILIATE: A local Southern Baptist Church participating in ACTS and paying a per capita fee for the ACTS satellite feed.

ACTS   AMERICAN CHRISTIAN TELEVISION SYSTEM: Satellite network of the Radio and Television Commission of the Southern Baptist Convention.

ARBITRON   One of the two leading US companies specialising in broadcast audience research (see Nielsen).

ARKLATEX   Region where Arkansas, Louisiana and Texas join.

AVN   ALTERNATE VIEW NETWORK: Based on First Methodist Church, Shreveport, Louisiana.

BACK-TO-BACK   One (religious) programme following another.

BBC   BRITISH BROADCASTING CORPORATION (or BOTT BROADCASTING COMPANY, Independence, Missouri).

BICYCLING   Distribution (of pre-recorded tapes) by post or special delivery, sometimes followed by redistribution to other studios. Bicycling is being superseded by satellite delivery.

BIRD   Satellite.

BTI   BRITISH TELECOM INTERNATIONAL.

BTN   BAPTIST   TELECOMMUNICATIONS   NETWORK (TelNeT): Southern Baptist Convention.

CATV   COMMUNITY ANTENNA TV: Cable television operations covering a large area (cf MATV).

CBN   THE   CHRISTIAN   BROADCASTING   NETWORK Inc.

CBNU   CBN UNIVERSITY.

CBS   COLUMBIA BROADCASTING SYSTEM.

CBT   CHRISTIAN BROADCAST TRAINING.

CHERRYPICKING   Choosing from the wide range of programming available from the various satellites.

CLEAR   Not encoded. Not scrambled. Not encrypted.

CTNA   CATHOLIC TELECOMMUNICATIONS NETWORK OF AMERICA.

CTVC   CHURCHES RADIO AND TELEVISION CENTRE.

CWR   CRUSADE FOR WORLD REVIVAL.

CWTV   CHRISTIAN WEEKEND TELEVISION.

DBS   DIRECT BROADCAST SATELLITE: Capable of reception in the home by small aerials/dishes (0.9-metre diameter).

DONOR BASE   The level of voluntary financial support for an individual or cause.

DOWNLINK   Communications signal from a satellite to the receiving TVRO (also used to describe the TVRO itself).

EBN   THE EUROPEAN BROADCASTING NETWORK.

ECS   EUROPEAN COMMUNICATIONS SATELLITE.

ELWA   Call-sign of Liberian-based Christian radio station.

ESA   EUROPEAN SPACE AGENCY.

EUTELSAT   The European telecommunications by satellite organisation.

EWTN   ETERNAL WORD TELEVISION NETWORK (Mother Angelica).

EXPLO   Satellite tele-conference of Campus Crusade for Christ.

EXPO   World Fair.

FACE   St FRANCIS ASSOCIATION FOR CATHOLIC EVANGELISM: Sponsors of the radio and television ministries of Father John Bertolucci.

FAIRNESS DOCTRINE   Places an 'affirmative obligation' on a broadcaster to cover controversial issues important to the community served, and to provide a reasonable opportunity for presentation of conflicting views. The Fairness Doctrine continues to be law. The FCC has released a study in which it concluded that the doctrine no longer serves the public interest.

FCC   FEDERAL COMMUNICATIONS COMMISSION.

FCCC   FEDERAL COUNCIL OF THE CHURCHES OF CHRIST IN THE USA: In 1950 it became the NCCC.

FRC   FEDERAL RADIO COMMISSION.

FOOTPRINT   Area of the earth's surface covered by the broadcast 'beam' of a satellite.

GIGAHERTZ   Term for the operating frequency of a satellite.

GEOSYNCHRONOUS (or GEOSTATIONARY)   Broadcast satellites are now 'parked' above the equator. As the earth rotates, they move at a speed which keeps them continually above the same position on the earth's surface. If the satellite could be viewed from the ground, it would be stationary.

IBA   INDEPENDENT BROADCASTING AUTHORITY.

INET   Meetings between the NCC, the Southern Baptist Convention, the US Catholic Conference and Jewish representatives on the one hand, and NBC and CBS on the other, to distribute religious public service airtime.

INTELSAT   International telecommunications by satellite organisation based in Washington.

ITP   INTERCOMMUNITY TELECOMMUNICATIONS PROJECT (Founding members: Paulist Fathers and Redemptorist Fathers and Brothers).

LOOK ANGLE   Alignment of a TVRO aerial towards a particular satellite.

LPTV   Low-power TV broadcast over a radius of up to 15 miles using a 100/1,000 watt transmitter.

MARKET   Notional subdivision of the US for particular commercial purposes.

MATV   MASTER ANTENNA TV: Communal (small-scale) cable TV operations.

MSO   MULTIPLE SYSTEM OPERATOR.

NASA   NATIONAL AERONAUTICS AND SPACE ADMINISTRATION.

NETWORK   NBC, CBS and ABC are the major American networks. They have been joined by the all-news CNN. Various religious broadcasting organisations describe themselves as 'networks'. Several deserve the title, but many of the smaller ones produce programmes for only part of the day and their coverage is potential rather than actual.

NCCC   NATIONAL COUNCIL OF THE CHURCHES OF CHRIST IN THE USA (formerly FCCC).

NIELSEN   The A.C. Nielsen Co is one of the two leading audience rating firms in the USA (see Arbitron).

NHI   NIELSEN HOMEVIDEO INDEX: Computer/ telephone system for rating cablevision programmes.

NPN   NATIONAL PARISH NETWORK.

NRB   NATIONAL RELIGIOUS BROADCASTERS.

NTI   NIELSEN TELEVISION INDEX: Computer/ telephone system for rating television programmes.

ORU   ORAL ROBERTS UNIVERSITY.

OVER-THE-AIR   Broadcasting from a transmitting antenna rather than over cable.

PBS   PUBLIC BROADCASTING SERVICE.

PIGGYBACKING   There are various meanings, one of which is to take up unused time on a satellite transponder— preferably between popular programmes.

PNCEA   PAULIST NATIONAL CATHOLIC EVANGE- LISATION ASSOCIATION.

PTL   PEOPLE THAT LOVE/INSPIRATION NET- WORK (Jim Bakker).

RTVC   THE RADIO AND TELEVISION COMMIS- SION: Southern Baptist Convention.

SATELLITE   Various meanings; but for present purposes, a man-made object that orbits the earth.

SBC   SOUTHERN BAPTIST CONVENTION.

SFC   SANTA FE COMMUNICATIONS.

SMATV   SATELLITE MASTER ANTENNA TV.

SPOT   SATELLITE POUR L'OBSERVATION DE TERRE.

STRONG-ARMING   Co-ordinated lobbying of a broad- casting company to transmit a particular programme or se- quence of programmes.

SUB-CARRIER   Broadcast signal included with another signal for another broadcasting purpose.

SUSTAINING TIME   Free air-time provided by a broad- casting company as a public service.

T-A-T   TELEVISION AWARENESS TRAINING.

TIMESHIFT   To transmit or view a broadcast at a later time (using a video recorder).

TRANSPONDER   Receiver/transmitter component of a satellite which receives a signal from earth and transmits it back to earth. Satellites can have 12–24 transponders.

TVRO TELEVISION RECEIVE ONLY: Earth station that magnifies the faint signal of a transmitting satellite for a TV set. It consists of the following components: dish, mount, feedhorn, low noise amplifier, feedline, receiver, modulator.

UHF ULTRA HIGH FREQUENCY.

UMCom UNITED METHODIST COMMUNICA-TIONS.

UNDA Latin for WAVE. Unda is the international Catholic broadcasters' association.

UPLINK Communications signal from the transmitting earth station to a satellite. It is also the name for the transmitting unit.

VCR VIDEO CASSETTE RECORDER.

VHF VERY HIGH FREQUENCY.

WACC WORLD ASSOCIATION FOR CHRISTIAN COMMUNICATION.

WASP WHITE ANGLO-SAXON PROTESTANT.

Off the Wire...News and Views

Electronic Church Is Booming

(George W. Cornell, A.P. Religion Writer, *New London Day,* January 31, 1987)

Ben Armstrong, executive director of National Religious Broadcasters, "says that growth [of the Electronic Church] is almost too fast to keep tabs on, amounting to an average of 20 new religious radio stations and two new religious television stations each month...

"At present, he reports there are 1,370 radio stations with full or substantial religious content in the country, up 22 percent in a decade, and 221 religious television stations, up 71 percent in five years."

Media Expenditures

(Steven Simpler, Religion Editor, *Arizona Republic,* October 1985)

Estimated annual media expenditures for USA's top five televangelists:

Pat Robertson	$ 233,000,000	Jim Bakker	$ 66,000,000
Jimmy Swaggart	$ 106,000,000	Oral Roberts	$ 60,000,000
Jerry Falwell	$ 100,000,000		

Falwell Scores on Tax Exemption

(The Washington Post, February 6, 1987)

The Rev. Jerry Falwell, seeking a property tax exemption worth millions of dollars on land he controls in Lynchburg [Virginia], won a skirmish yesterday in the state Senate and seemed poised for another legislative victory today.

By a 27-to-13 vote, the Senate kept alive a proposal that would exempt Falwell's Old Time Gospel Hour Inc. from $1,400,000 in back taxes, interest, and penalties that has built up since 1979, when Falwell stopped paying local taxes.

Falwell's refusal to pay taxes on about 260 acres owned by Old Time Gospel Hour and used primarily by Liberty University became a test of wills as well as a court battle with Lynchburg City officials, who at first insisted that he was ineligible for the tax exemption.

However, the city changed its position last year after Falwell threatened to move his operations to Atlanta unless the exemption were granted. Falwell's operations employ several thousand people in the Lynchburg area. . . .

Oral Roberts' Peers Critical of Campaign

Maureen McDonald and Cheryl Mattox Berry, *USA TODAY,* February 3, 1987)

TV evangelist Oral Roberts has crossed the line of good faith with recent pleas for money, some religious broadcasters say.

"It was emotional blackmail," radio station manager Linda Tierman of St. Louis, Mo., said Sunday. Added radio producer Hector Bezarees of Port Charlotte, Fla.: "I look on this with disdain."

Roberts told viewers of his TV show *Expect a Miracle* that God will end his life in March [1987] unless he raises $4.5 million.

Roberts declined to appear before the 4,000 attending the 44th annual National Religious Broadcasters convention in Washington, D.C. The group is trying to arrange a satellite interview with Roberts' spokesman, his son Richard.

Religious broadcasting is the fastest-growing segment of broadcasting in the USA. Currently there are 1,370 radio and 221 TV stations with full or substantial religious content.

Today President Reagan addresses the convention in a videotaped message. Vice President Bush will speak afterward in person.

Perspectives

(Pat Robertson, CBN President, *Newsweek,* February 2, 1987)

"Oral is a dear friend and I support him all the way, but I was still amazed. I never thought God would hold someone accountable for not raising money."

Electronic Religion

(American Demographics, August 1986)

Forty-five percent of Americans watch religious programs on television or listen to them on radio at least monthly, according to an ABC/ Washington Post poll. Nine percent watch or listen daily. No wonder religion is big business.

The listenership is even higher among Protestants. Eighty-six percent of black Protestants and 58% of white Protestants say they watch or listen to electronic religious programs at least once a month. Twenty-eight percent of black Protestants, 12 percent of white Protestants, and 5 percent of Catholics do so daily.

The share of people who attend religious services from their living rooms is about the same as the share who go to church. While 34 percent of Americans go to church weekly, 33 percent say they listen or watch religious services at least weekly.

Black Protestants are more likely to attend services at home than at church. Seventy-five percent said they watch or listen to services daily or weekly. Among white Protestants, 56 percent go to church weekly, while 44 percent listen or watch religious services at least weekly

...While 54 percent of Catholics attend church weekly, only 22 percent tune into electronic religion each week.

Christian Broadcasting Network High in Violence

(John Butler, *Our Sunday Visitor,* January 25, 1987)

Violence on television and its potentially harmful effects on children and teenagers are issues that never seem to go away....

Moreover, according to the National Coalition on Television Violence (NCTV), many of these violent acts can be viewed on CBN, a network owned and operated by Evangelist Pat Robertson and which advertises itself as "the family entertainer."

"I find it distressing that the world's largest Christian television network carries a majority of the top cable shows that are high in violence," says Dr. Thomas Radecki, a psychiatrist and research director of NCTV. "Unfortunately, right now the most popular programs on CBN are more violent than the most popular television shows on the CBS television network.". . .

After CBN president Pat Robertson said that his network aired the most popular family entertainment on cable television, NCTV began a deeper look at the programming content. Volunteers studied more than 100 hours of CBN shows, examining the number of violent acts in each program.

Much to the surprise of the coalition, the monitors found that CBN programming contained about 34 violent acts per hour, and about 35 of the 43 hours of action-adventure programming each week appeared to be the kind that is "likely to teach violence" as the best way to solve problems.

"I do not believe that CBN should air one single hour of violent programming, but it is shocking to see some 35 hours a week of violence on a Christian network," says Radecki.

The coalition also found that, from a Christian perspective, the programming "portrayed opponents as stereotypic, one-dimensional villains with no redeeming qualities. These programs made no attempt to teach one of love one's enemy or to resist evil with good.". . .

The Christian Right: Will It Bring Political Pentecost to America?

(Clifford Goldstein, *Liberty* November/December 1986)

Across America, conservative Christians are flexing political muscle. By mobilizing volunteers, registering voters, lobbying, forming PACs, raising funds, publishing literature, purchasing television time, and supporting or even running candidates, the evangelical movement. . .has become the undisputed heavyweight of American neo-conservatism.

Its goals, too, are nothing short of Olympian. Says New Right chieftain Paul Weyrich, "We want to govern America."

Pat Robertson, for one, is willing to cooperate. He seeks nothing less than the presidency—deferring his official candidacy until September, 1987, however, enables him to continue his ministry and public exposure on his 700 Club....

Now, however, a segment of the evangelicals are engaged in a new ministry, one that's alien from the commission Christ left His church. The prominence of pastors Jerry Falwell, James Robison, and W.A. Chriswell in influencing sections of the 1984 Republican convention platform is one example of the New Right's growing political, if not spiritual, muscle. Their decisive influence in local Republican organizations is another. The Reagan administration's support of government-sponsored prayer in school is another. Appointments of hundreds of fundamentalists to government posts are another. And now we have a New Right candidate campaigning for the presidency!...

Running for President?

(Televangelist Rev. Pat Robertson, Constitution Hall, Philadelphia, September 17, 1986)

"If by September 17, 1987, three million registered voters have signed petitions telling me they will pray— that they will work—that they will give toward my election, then I will run as a candidate for the nomination of the Republican Party for the Office of the President of the United States."

(A fund-raising letter, intended to reach followers the next day, asked those who signed the petition to give $100 toward the effort. *Christianity in Crisis,* November 17, 1986)

Secretary Bennet Replies

(Response by William Bennet, Secretary U.S. Dept. of Education, to Pat Robertson's views on patriotism quoted in *Christianity and Crisis,* November 17, 1986)

"A public figure recently said Christians feel more strongly about love of country, love of God, and support for the traditional family than do non-Christians.

"This sort of invidious sectarianism must be renounced in the strongest terms. The vibrant families and warm patriotism of millions upon millions of non-Christians and nonreligious Americans give it the lie."

The Robertson Candidacy

(David Earle Anderson, UPI religion and social issues writer, *Christianity and Crisis,* November 17, 1986)

...On the day after [Robertson's] announcement, syndicated columnist Cal Thomas, once a key aide to Jerry Falwell, reported that Falwell told him: "I'm not going to get involved anymore in campaigns as I have in the past." While not disavowing George Bush (whom he strongly supported earlier) nor rushing to endorse Robertson, Falwell's action — if it holds — removes Robertson's most potent rival for political leadership of the conservative evangelical-fundamentalist constituency.

Robert Grant, head of the increasingly influential Christian Voice and formerly a personal supporter of Rep. Jack Kemp (R-N.Y.), has also suggested the entire evangelical movement needs to back Robertson — at least for now.

The most dramatic — and controversial — convert to Robertson's cause has been the flamboyant,

charismatic Baton Rouge, La., evangelist, Jimmy Swaggart.

Swaggart, like Falwell, leaned early to frontrunner Bush, who has been heavily courting the religious right since he took office. But in early September, Swaggart stunned his colleagues by announcing Support for the Robertson candidacy. And he made his announcement with the typical Swaggart flair: "For the first time in human history, the possibility exists that the hand that is laid on the Holy Bible will be joined to a shoulder, a head, and a heart that are saved by the Lord Jesus Christ and filled with the Holy Spirit."

For Robertson, Swaggart support could well prove to be something of a double-edged sword — a boon in the rural white South where Swaggart's popularity is strong and his revivals draw thousands. But in other places, where his extremist, anti-

Catholic, anti-Jewish views are anathema, it could prove to be a real embarrassment. Already Swaggart is being compared to Louis Farrakhan, the outspoken Black Muslim leader who was such a deterrent to support for Jesse Jackson in 1984....

For now, Robertson is pursuing a twofold political strategy. First, he wants to build a solid organization based on the fundamentalist-evangelical constituency, including at least a public united front with the oft-times fractious and sometimes jealous leadership of the theologically diverse movement. Second, he wants to reassure the regulars, like Bennet, primarily through stressing secular elements of his past and present (such as his familial ties to Virginia politics; his father was Sen. Willis Robertson, D-Va.), his graduation from Yale Law School, and his role as a businessman in the huge, multi-million-dollar CBN empire....

Back-Handed Endorsement

(America, January 10, 1987)

Television evangelist Jimmy Swaggart says he has endorsed the Rev. Pat Robertson for President because he never really felt his fellow Christian broadcaster had "the calling of God" to be either a pastor or a preacher. According to the Religious News Service, the fiery Baton Rouge, La., evangelist made the remark in explaining to followers why, after so many years of railing against ministers in politics, he gave his much-sought-after endorsement in September to Mr. Robertson. The endorsement by Mr. Swaggart also is viewed as furthering the crumbling alliance between Vice President George Bush and his principal supporter in the evangelical world, the Rev. Jerry Falwell. Writing in The Evangelist, his ministry's monthly magazine, Mr. Swaggart said he has not changed is mind about preachers aspiring to public office, asserting, "I have never seen any good come of it."

Robertson Tests the Candidate Voice

(Phil Gailey, Special to *The New York Times,* February 12, 1987)

..."I've been told Ronald Reagan won the New Hampshire primary in 1980 with 34,000 votes," he said, glancing at an aide for confirmation. "Let me tell you there's nothing impossible about this."...

Mr. Robertson contended that the Iran arms sales controversy that has enveloped the Reagan Administration had 'dramatically' altered the Republican contest, primarily by undermining Vice President Bush's position and making political integrity a major concern.

"The best politicians in 1988 may well be the nonpolitician," Mr. Robertson said with a smile.

Robertson Gain Seen in Michigan

(Richard L. Berke, Special to *The New York Times,* February 15, 1987)

Strategists for Vice President Bush, acknowledging that they overestimated their candidate's strength, now concede that the Rev. Pat Robertson won nearly as many delegates as the Vice President in the state's precinct voting last August.

The August contest, electing Republican delegates from precincts to go to county meetings, was the first in the nation that will have a direct bearing on the allocation of delegates to the Republican National Convention in 1988....

"There is a very positive victory for us," Mr. Robertson said of the Michigan delegate count. "It looks as if we'll have 50 percent of the delegates at the state convention. You can draw your own conclusion, but to me it's pretty startling."

Excerpts from *Prophecy and Politics: Militant Evangelists on the Road to Nuclear War* by Grace Halsell (Westport, Conn.: Lawrence Hill & Company, 1986)

I find a vast difference between the fundamentalism of my childhood and the fundamentalism of today. In my childhood, preachers often denounced movies, dancing, whisky and evolution. Brother Turner and even J. Frank Norris had only limited funds and they did not have television and there was no state of Israel — that is, no official site for an Armageddon. Most important, there was no atomic bomb. Today [Jerry] Falwell, Pat Robertson and other dispensationalists seemingly have unlimited

financial resources. They have a battle site in Israel and a line of reasoning for a nuclear war—God wills it. And they preach, promote and actually sell Americans on the idea of building more bombs and then using them.

The preachers in my childhood, advancing their belief in the Virgin Birth of Christ and God's creation in six days of the universe, were dealing with events of the past. And thus they presented no menace to our existence. Like apocalyptic Marxists, Falwell and other fundamentalists today have embraced a cult of *their* scenario of our future. And since the dispensationalists say our future lies in war and annihilation, they pose a danger entirely different and more far-reaching than that of the earlier evangelicals and fundamentalists.... [p.197]

...an Israeli public opinion poll published in 1984 [showed] that 18.7 percent of the Israeli public support terrorist activities by extremist Jewish groups. In commenting on the poll, the Israeli writer Yehoehus Sobol pointed out that in 1938, a representative sample of the Nazi Party members found that 63 percent of them objected to hurting Jews, 32 percent expressed apathy on the subject and only five percent were in favor of harming Jews.

Four years later, in 1942, when the annihilation of Jews was already speedily taking place, a representative sampling of the Nazi Party members showed that those against attacking Jews decreased to 26 percent, while the number of apathetic increased to 69 percent. The number of Nazi in favor of attacking Jews remained the same: five percent.

"It is clear," Sobol said, "that during the activation of the policy of genocide toward the Jewish people, only five percent of the Nazi Party members were prepared to identify with the policy....Now after 50 years, there is no justification anymore for ignoring a danger that is embodied in a fragmented-fanatic minority. A careful examination of the distribution of the views and positions in German society in the Nazi period has left no excuse for anyone today to claim that as long as racist ideas belong only to a small minority, there is no basis on which to speak about the fascistization of the whole society.... [pp.115-116]

The extremists among the Israeli Jews are still not a majority, and the Christian extremists are still not a majority. However, I have attempted to show that the alliance between these right-wing, militaristic groups gives both a quantum leap in real, unsentimental power and might. Moreover, leaders in both groups are obsessed with their own belief system, their own ideology, their own certitude that they have both the right and the power to help orchestrate not only their own End of Times, but doomsday for the rest of the species.... [p.200]